MIND AND LIFE

AN ESSAY IN SIMPLIFICATION

A. G. TANSLEY

MIND AND LIFE

AN ESSAY IN SIMPLIFICATION

LONDON
GEORGE ALLEN & UNWIN LTD
RUSKIN HOUSE · MUSEUM STREET

PRINTED IN GREAT BRITAIN
in 13 point Perpetua type
BY SIMSON SHAND LTD
LONDON AND HERTFORD

PREFACE

THIS BOOK represents a modest attempt to pick out for consideration certain topics whose discussion seems to me to throw light on the nature and working of the mind and its place in human life, to try to isolate a few guiding threads from the infinitely complex web of existing knowledge and speculation about the mind. It also of course represents fragments of a personal philosophy.

In this endeavour two modes of approach have been largely used—the biological and the psycho-analytic. It seems to me that no psychology (or philosophy either) can be valid unless it is in substantial accords with biological facts and principles (so far as these are relevant) because our minds and our reasoning powers as well as our instincts and emotions are based upon man as a biological organism. They have emerged in the course of evolution from less complex and less specialized processes in preceding organisms from which we are descended, and their nature and limitations cannot be understood unless a continuing hold is kept on their biological basis. Too many philosophers and not a few psychologists seem to assume implicitly (though they might be the first to deny any such assumption) that the human intellect is a more or less perfect reasoning mechanism, which can be trusted to work satisfactorily and to arrive at valid conclusions in detachment from its biological antecedents. Man is after all primarily an animal, whatever else he may be, and no concentration of attention on his unique powers and achievements can alter the fact and its consequences. The only way of escape from this conclusion is by assuming that man's mental and spiritual faculties have been, as it were, 'plastered on' to a pre-existing animal, by denying, in effect, the reality of the evolution of the human organism as a whole.

A recent historical writer[1] has stressed 'the attitude of the historian as distinct from that of the biologist. . . . The historian . . . does not regard him (man) as essentially a part of nature or consider him primarily in this aspect . . . he envisages a world of human relations standing, so to speak, over against nature'. This attitude is doubtless inevitable for the historian in his professional capacity, but it is dangerous in any general consideration of human behaviour. Professor Butterfield makes the necessary admission when he writes: 'It may be true that nature and history are not separable in the last resort, but (he continues) it is important not to synthesize them too easily and too soon.' From the standpoint of fundamental analysis however it is not a question of 'synthesis' at all. We must recognize at the outset that man *is* an animal, in other words biology comes first, psychology next, and history last, though in his own field the historian has to deal primarily with the behaviour of mankind through the ages, and the psychologist with the causes of that behaviour. And if we are to remain content, as Professor Butterfield suggests, 'to regard the world of men as a thing apart, to envisage a world of human relations set up against nature and the animal kingdom' without examining the very foundation of the whole, it may certainly 'have the effect of transforming any impression that we may finally acquire concerning the universe as a whole', but we shall as certainly misconceive human nature altogether, and that will not be a very sound step in the process of acquiring impressions about the universe.

The psycho-analytical formulations in this book are used because in my judgment they have given us an altogether fresh and essential insight into the basic nature of the human mind as it actually works. It has been unnecessary for my purpose to bring in anything like the whole of current psychoanalytical theory, though a chapter is devoted to considering

[1] Professor Butterfield in *Christianity and History*, 1949, pp. 6, 7.

the strength and weakness of the movement and of some of the doctrines involved. It is interesting to note the strongly contrasting attitudes of eminent current writers towards psycho-analytical doctrines. Many of them are evidently convinced of the truth and value of their essential basis, others are as clearly irritated by psycho-analysis, and often become rather peevish in their allusions to the subject. This latter attitude partly reflects the inherent weakness of a good deal of psycho-analytical speculation, and the depressing effect of the multiplication of technical terminology—commonly referred to as 'jargon'—but it seems likely to be partly due also to a concealed fear that at least some of the doctrines may be valid and a profound dislike of their implications. One curious argument sometimes used by distinguished literary critics is that psycho-analysis of a work of art destroys the power of aesthetic appreciation of a poem, drama or picture. Do these critics really believe, for example, that botanical knowledge of the detailed structure and mode of working of the parts of a flower destroys or impairs appreciation of its beauty? The two functions of the mind—scientific investigation and aesthetic appreciation—are of course quite different in nature, but neither need interfere in any way with the other. On the contrary, as Wordsworth knew, they are capable of reinforcing each other.

Another not uncommon attitude tending to depreciate the status of psycho-analysis is to concede the value of the medical use of analysis, but to deny, explicitly or implicitly, its application to the 'normal' mind. Yet it is abundantly clear that no sharp line can be drawn between the 'normal' and the psycho-neurotic mind, the latter being a mind in which the adjusted balance of mental health is impaired, so that conflicts which are normally under control become distressingly apparent in the form of mental or physical 'symptoms'. In a mild form many of these are evident enough in the

most normally adjusted person, for few if any mental adjustments can be ideally perfect. If psycho-analytical formulations have any validity at all they apply to the basic structure
and the basic mechanisms of the human mind, at least to the
instinctive and emotional structure and mechanisms. The
discoveries on which the formulations are based were made,
it is true, in psycho-neurotic patients: that was because the
motive forces at work could, in the first instance, only be
seen clearly when they were more or less isolated and thrown
into prominence by disturbance of the normal balance.

Neither the biological nor the psycho-analytic approach to
psychology implies that the higher human values are not real
values in their own right, nor do they exclude the possibility
of an ultimate spiritual reality.

The topics dealt with do not include any aspects of psychopathology as such, and the 'seamy' side of human nature is
for the most part neglected. Considering the abundant literature that now exists on such topics, however, no reader is
likely to be wholly ignorant of the psycho-analytic mechanisms, of that intricate mixture of good and evil, of constructive and destructive impulses, which is characteristic of
human beings.

Since the plan of the book is to pick out certain topics
which can be examined more or less separately, a good deal
of simplification—some readers may think over-simplification
—as well as restatement of theses which may be regarded as
truisms—some readers may feel to the point of banality—is
involved, and much that would have to be included in any
attempt at a comprehensive picture of the mind is neglected
altogether. But this method of treatment is deliberate, and
at least the confusion that so often results from attempts to
deal with complexities which cannot be clearly analysed or
grasped in single expositions is avoided.

No apology is made for the prominence given to Mc-

Dougall's conception of human instinct as the basis of a large part of psychical activity. Unfashionable ('outmoded') as this approach has become among certain modern schools of social psychology the author is convinced that so far from being obsolete or obsolescent it is still indispensable. On the other hand, the wide range of modern techniques of thought and formulation which fall under the general heading of 'field theory', highly valuable as they undoubtedly are in both physical and psychological science, have been left on one side because they are not specially useful in considering the particular limited problems dealt with in the following pages.

It is scarcely necessary to say that no claim is made to originality. Probably every idea in the book has already been put forward by someone, from Aristotle to the latest writer on psychology or logical analysis, and no documentation beyond a few incidental references to the literature has been attempted.

Acknowledgment of help given by two friends is gratefully made. Dr Harry Godwin has been good enough to read the typescript and make useful comments, while Professor Harold Jeffreys has helped to clear up some difficult points dealt with in the first part of Chapter 6.

A. G. T.

CONTENTS

CHAPTER 1

BODY, MIND AND SPIRIT

EVERY HUMAN being is necessarily vividly conscious of the existence of his own body. It is the most familiar thing in the world, the instrument he uses in whatever he does. But the very fact that he calls it *his* body means that he does not regard it as the whole of himself—that there is something more, a something to which his body *belongs*. When a man thinks of himself as a *person*, with his own individual sensations, thoughts, feelings and will, it is not of his body that he thinks first, though he would not exist—at least here on earth—if it were not for his body. He himself, the person, thinks of his body as something distinct from his *self*, though an indispensable part of it. He cannot avoid recognizing that there is something in him concerned with thinking, feeling and suffering, something responsible too for his will. The activity of this something precedes all his actions except those which are automatic and normally unconscious, like breathing and digestion, and those which are 'reflex' and automatic in response to an external stimulus, like blinking in a sudden bright light. This other part of himself he calls his *mind*, and it is often conveniently called his *psyche*.[1]

The mind is not visible or tangible like the body, it is not extended in space, but it is none the less 'real'.[2] To make any

1 The concept of 'mind' is restricted by some writers to the *thinking* part of the organism, and the 'psyche' is sometimes taken as concerned with a sphere considered as intermediate between mind in this sense and body, i.e. with the instincts and emotions that are bound up with obvious physiological processes, and are thus closer to the body than thinking and reasoning. But there is no uniformity of precisely defined usages of these terms and in this book 'mind' and 'psyche' are treated as almost synonymous.

2 There are, however, some extreme 'behaviourists' who deny that the concept of 'mind' should have any place in scientific psychology and would wish to abolish it altogether.

sort of picture of the working of the individual human life is impossible unless we recognize that it is dominated by a set of functions distinct from the bodily functions. It used often to be said that the brain is the organ of mind just as the lungs are the organs of breathing. It is perfectly true that the brain is the seat of the central physiological processes which accompany what we call perception and thought, and that without those processes thought could not be initiated or carried on. But we cannot locate the mind in space within the body: the brain is only the primary material mechanism through which the mind works. In the brain tissue are made the combinations of stimuli coming from the sense organs and the viscera, which result in mental 'perceptions', with the physical records in the brain tissue corresponding with 'memory traces' of earlier perceptions and thoughts; and these combinations form the necessary physical basis of thought and emotion.

Thought itself is something of a completely different nature from the functions of any bodily organ. Together with the feelings thought creates a sphere, the sphere of personal consciousness, distinct from the bodily functions and identifiable with what has been called the 'empirical ego', the self of which we are immediately conscious.

The mind has a kind of universal relation to the body as a whole and to all the different parts of the body. It can affect, and in its turn be affected by, every bodily organ and function. We all know that when we are in perfect health our minds are apt to be at their best, and that when we are ill or our bodily condition is poor the mind seldom works satisfactorily. We also know that happiness and contentment have an excellent general effect on bodily health, and that persistent mental depression or definite mental illness will often lead to more or less grave deterioration of our bodily functions. Any defect in the functioning of an organ, whether it amounts to what we recognize as disease or not, may affect the mind, not by affecting the brain tissue detrimentally but directly, though the action of the central nervous system is often involved. And changes in the functioning of the mind, however caused, may react directly upon the body and any of its functions.

But alongside these close interdependences the mind has a considerable *independence*, in fact an essential autonomy of its own. A man of very poor general physique *may* have an excellent and excellently functioning mind. In some severe physical illnesses the mind remains remarkably clear and may work with unaccustomed facility. States of robust physical health and vigour do not always conduce to mental activity.

An experienced American psychiatrist[1] remarks that 'when disease or disorder of any organ affects the mind, the seriousness of the effect depends upon the *strength of the mind*. When this is strongly organized it does not succumb easily'. The absence of any exact correlation and often of any clear connection at all between disease or disorder of brain and mind is brought out by two further remarks of the same authority. 'There is no location in the brain or any other part of the body in which a uniform group of mental symptoms originates. A brain tumour may cause quite different symptoms according to the personality and its psychopathic[2] trends.' More mental troubles appear 'in the guise of stomach disorders than of neurological[3] disturbances'. Again, when a mental disorder directly induces a physical disorder, as when certain hysterical states lead to the paralysis of a limb or part of a limb, the bodily symptom does not follow the lines of any nerve distribution but is located according to a purely mental connection with the part of the body paralysed. There can scarcely be more convincing evidence of the direct universal relation of mind and body independent of the working of the nervous system.

Mental processes are functions of the entire organism— mind has indeed been called a 'process that goes on in living

[1] Mental physician.   [2] Relating to disorder of the mind.
[3] Relating to the nervous system.

matter', or in other words 'psychological processes are functions of biological systems'. But we can say nothing about the nature of mental process in terms of physiological process or of *how* either can affect the other. It is this distinctness of mental process from any other sort of living process that led to the old conception of mind as something dwelling within the body, like a man living in a house[1]. But this is no longer a possible way of regarding the mind.

The body has material substance and definiteness of outline, a clear distinctness from the rest of the sensory world: furthermore its various functions can often be analysed and described in terms of physical and chemical processes. For all these reasons it is natural and inevitable to regard the body as a physical entity. From the point of view of the organism as a whole the mind, on the other hand, is a complex of interlocking functions, of quite distinct and specific nature, which cannot be described and analysed in physical and chemical terms; and it is this fact of course that has led to the existence of psychology as a separate branch of science.

When physical or mental disorder overtakes us the cause may be in either case physical or mental, but very commonly both together. A bacterial infection may cause a severe disease, with or without serious repercussions on the mind, and psychical depression is often a cause of the lack of resistance which enables the bacteria or virus to make headway. A purely mental upset may, as we saw, have a direct effect on the body, but on the other hand the physical health may remain good in spite of a severe mental disturbance. For these reasons psychiatrists distinguish between somatogenic[2] and psychogenic[3] symptoms, whether the symptoms themselves are physical or mental. One of the most important results of psychiatric work during the last half century has been the increasing recognition that many severe bodily symptoms are

---

[1] This conception was long held to be perfectly valid for the 'soul'.
[2] Originating in the body.   [3] Originating in the mind.

psychogenic. Patient after patient comes to a general practitioner or to a specialist in a branch of physical medicine complaining of some persistent bodily trouble. The physician can find nothing organically wrong, and only when a psychiatrist has been consulted is it discovered that the cause of the physical symptom is some mental trouble, nearly always ultimately traceable to a serious mental disturbance which occurred in the patient's past history and which often directly or indirectly involved the part of the body in which the symptom has appeared.

Regarded as a particular complex of *functions* of the organism as a whole—and from one point of view we must so regard it—mind cannot well be conceived of as 'interacting' with the body, which is clearly a material thing, but in practice we have also to consider the mind as an entity which is largely autonomous, an entity which is immaterial but in which we can distinguish *structure*. We cannot see the structure nor touch its parts, but we must assume their existence, or rather we must construct a working model of the mind as a mental picture in order to analyse mental activities and relate them to one another. In this task the psychology of the last half century has had considerable success, so that great advances in our knowledge of the nature of mind have been made possible.

But besides his body and mind man has traditionally (and nearly always) conceived of another immaterial entity, his *soul* or *spirit*, which has been, and commonly is, held to survive the death and disintegration of his body. We need not here discuss the question of how the idea of the soul arose in the course of the evolution of man's mind from that of his ape-like ancestors. The point is that he has never been able to escape, at least during recent millennia, from the conception of soul or spirit as part of his being, the conviction, as Aldous Huxley puts it in his book, *The Perennial Philosophy*, that 'there exists some kind of permanent soul by which experience is organized and which in turn makes use of that organized experience to become a particular and unique personality'. This, as Huxley says, is a tenet of orthodox Hinduism (though not of Buddhism), and of almost all European philosophical and religious thought from Aristotle onwards—'all exponents of the Perennial Philosophy make, in one form or another, the affirmation that man is a kind of trinity composed of body, psyche and spirit'[1]. 'Nature' may say, in Tennyson's words, 'the spirit doth but mean the breath, I know no more', and it is very doubtful how far we can deal with spirit as such by the methods of natural science. There are many indeed today who would deny the existence of spirit as a separate entity, and would attribute the supposed spiritual activities of man to particular functions of his mind. We have seen that on the plane of natural science mind is correctly regarded in the first place as the aggregate of functions of a particular kind in the organism as a whole, but that it must also be regarded as an entity in its own right which we can investigate by scientific methods and in which we can recognize structure. In the same way it is possible to look upon spirit as a particular and specialized kind of mental function; and it is also possible to regard it as an entity in its own right. But if we make the assumption (or are led to the conclusion) that spirit is a separate active entity in its own right, can we investigate its manifestations by the methods of natural science?

During the last three-quarters of a century a great deal of investigation has been made of what are now called 'paranormal' phenomena, in this country notably by the Society for Psychical Research; and some of it, especially in America but also in Britain, with the use of strict laboratory controls. Of the objective existence of such phenomena, which cannot be 'explained' in terms of any kind of recognized psychology,

[1] This division omits the mind as such. The functions of what is called the mind in this book, and commonly in modern psychological writing, would be divided by Huxley between 'psyche' and 'spirit'.

no unbiased observer can now entertain reasonable doubt. Putting aside all cases in which fraud is suspected (and there have of course been many experiments in which fraud has not only been suspected but proved), as well as all doubtful results, there remain a great number of occurrences which are 'facts' in precisely the same sense as that in which normal phenomena of the physical world, observed by competent and trustworthy people, are facts. To a certain extent tentative conclusions can be drawn about the relations of these paranormal facts to one another and to living persons, but nevertheless we cannot at present regard 'psychical research' as a branch of natural science, because the paranormal facts are so completely out of relation with the general body of natural knowledge, nor has it been possible to construct any coherent and intelligible theory of the working of paranormal phenomena even within a separate sphere. Endowed as we are with minds evolved in close adaptation to our vital need for perceiving and acting upon the material world around us it is not difficult to conceive that if there is another world, interdigitating, so to speak, with the familiar material and mental worlds, but which does not normally affect our dealings with the material and the mental, we should have no adequate powers of understanding or dealing with it. There may possibly be a large number of different kinds of paranormal processes, some of which directly concern the individual human personality—the human spirit—while some do not. All such processes are difficult—perhaps impossible—to grasp clearly with our limited human intelligence; and this might still be true even if we knew much more of the facts than we do.

But there may be other means of access to some of them, and of these the oldest and most fundamental is through religion, which insists on the reality and immortality of the human spirit.

In the sphere of religion we can identify the spirit with the conception of the soul,[1] regarded in the Christian religion, for instance, as immortal and as securing the survival of the personality after the death of the body. With the advent of Christianity the idea of the soul was directly connected with the Christian God. It had no meaning except in relation to God. The nature of the soul in its relation to God is essentially a metaphysical and theological problem inaccessible to the methods of analysis used by natural science.

But whether or not we accept the account of the soul given by Christian theologians we cannot escape from the psychological reality of spiritual *values*,[2] and the soul is the traditional name for the spiritual part of man which deals in those values. To the religious man the soul and not the mind is the essential core of the individual: it is the soul that has to be saved or damned, and the soul is quite independent of the physical body, as the mind or psyche, in spite of its relative autonomy, is not.

[1] Some religious writers identify the soul with what we are calling the mind or psyche and distinguish the spirit as the highest part of man, so that the human trinity becomes body, soul and spirit. But here we are taking human soul and human spirit as synonymous.

[2] Considered in the final chapter.

CHAPTER 2

THE STRUCTURE OF THE MIND

WE SAW in the last chapter that mind can be thought of as the aggregate of those functions of the human organism which we call mental and which are roughly divisible into perception, thought and emotion: to these must be added *conation* or 'set' of the mind towards action. But this aggregate, as we have seen, comes to have an independence and an individuality of its own, so that it must also be thought of as an entity in its own right.

The body furnishes the material basis on and through which the mind works, and apart from this primary relation the mind is constantly influenced by the body and the bodily functions. Nevertheless the mind has an autonomy that cannot be gainsaid. It exerts an important influence on the body and its functions and normally has direct control of a large part of the activity of the entire organism.

When we think of the mind we usually and most naturally think solely of our conscious mind. Many people indeed, even some philosophers, will not admit the possibility that any other part of the mind can exist. Mental processes, they say, cannot be other than conscious—that is directly implied by the word 'mental': all unconscious processes are necessarily non-mental. Of course if we choose to define 'mental' in this way the statement is a truism or tautology. But during the last half century psychologists, or most of them, have become convinced that we must assume the existence of an unconscious part of the mind if we would begin to understand the functioning of the mind as a whole. And acceptance of this conclusion is shared by most lay authors who touch upon the subject and who commonly write of the 'subconscious mind'.

The abundant evidence for the existence of the subconscious mind will not be dealt with here. Its cogency becomes apparent directly we try to analyse the behaviour of the mind as a whole by psycho-analytic methods; and these have in fact given us a wholly fresh insight into that behaviour, and a self-consistent picture of the mind.

It is obvious that our moment-to-moment consciousness does not include all the material at the mind's disposal, but only a small fraction of it. What we think of at any instant of time commonly, though by no means invariably, concerns what we are doing or meditating upon at the moment, whether it be physical or mental work, reading a book, playing an instrument or a game, talking with other people, contemplating a picture or a landscape, or making love. The thing with which we are immediately concerned is brought into the focus of consciousness, a process which has been compared with the throwing of a spotlight upon a particular area of mental material. There is much else, easily accessibly to consciousness, which is not in the focus at any given moment, such for instance as stored knowledge, the results of past experience which remain 'in the memory'—in effect everything that can be remembered and called upon when it is wanted. All such accessible mental material is called *pre-conscious* by psycho-analysts, the equivalent of Freud's *Vorbewusste*.

But beyond the preconscious there is other mental material which is not easily accessible to consciousness. Some of this material can only be brought into the focus with great difficulty and by the use of special methods, but it can often be shown to have a great and continuous effect on the mind as a whole, and not only upon the mind but upon the 'vegetative' organs of the body, though of the existence of this effect, and of its origin, we are normally quite unaware. Such material is essentially *mental* in nature, as is obvious when it becomes conscious and must therefore be regarded as belonging to the unconscious mind, or, as it is called by psycho-analysts, simply the *unconscious* (*Unbewusste*). Most people go through life in complete ignorance of the existence of their unconscious minds, let alone of what they contain. It was the work of Freud and his followers that established the existence of the unconscious and its profound significance in human life.[1] The word 'subconscious', which is commonly used by lay writers but not much by psychologists, usually refers to the unconscious, though we may if we like include in its meaning both the preconscious and the unconscious, since both lie outside and, as it were, 'below' the normal, moment-to-moment, consciousness.[2] Such a use however, tends to blur the profound difference between the easily accessible preconscious and the very recondite unconscious material.

Still, though there is a profound difference, there is no completely sharp limit between preconscious and unconscious. There are things in our minds which we are far from being easily able to make fully conscious, but of which nevertheless we have some inkling, and these may be thought of as lying in the border zone between preconscious and unconscious. The process of psycho-analysis is directed to the task of raising particular contents of the unconscious up to the focus of consciousness. If it is successful the material remains for the future in the preconscious when it is not being actually thought of.

The contents of the unconscious appear to be of two kinds. First there is mental material involved in the nature and action of what are often called the primitive *instincts*, but which in this context are perhaps better called by the rather ugly though vigorously expressive names of 'drives' or 'urges'. The

[1] The idea of the existence of an unconscious part of the mind had been familiar to many thinkers long before Freud; but it was he who firmly established its existence by evidence that can fairly be called scientific and began to analyse its contents and modes of action.

[2] The spatial metaphor is almost impossible to avoid. We naturally think of the 'fully lighted' consciousness as 'above' the preconscious material not actually in the spotlight, and of the dark recesses of the unconscious as more deeply buried.

problem of instinct is considered in Chapter 5, and it will be enough here if we refer to two universal human characters which are commonly called instincts, namely the instinct of self preservation[1] and that of sex. These universal motives of many human actions are clearly primary in the human organism, for if we lacked them neither the individual nor the race could survive. The sex instinct and at least some of the activities of self preservation are rooted in physiological processes, largely the effects on the body of glandular secretions formed in response to particular stimuli and acting as *hormones*[2] which bring about changes of the bodily state and consequent specific actions. But these physiological processes have accompanying mental representations, and it is these chains of processes which have physiological roots and also mental expressions, that constitute the most characteristic and undeniable human instincts or 'drives'.

We cannot give any account of the actual relation between these closely connected physiological and psychical processes, for we have no means of analysing the nature of the transitions between the bodily and the mental. In the working of any primary instinct the two constantly act and interact and seem to pass imperceptibly one into the other. A pressing danger or an attractive sexual object is perceived and both physiological and psychical reactions immediately result. The working of the instinct is a whole, emphasizing the essential unity or integration of the physical and mental functions of the organism. The mental part of the instinctive work is primarily unconscious, though the exciting sensory stimuli (the danger or the sexual object) are vivid enough in consciousness, and *it is the aggregate of the mental components of all the primary instincts that forms the basis of the unconscious mind.*

[1] The preservation of the self from imminent danger, which can be distinguished from the general principle of 'self-maintenance' dealt with in Chapter 3.

[2] Definite chemical substances whose liberation into the blood stream initiates particular sets of physiological processes.

This primary basis of the mind is now called by psycho-analysts the *id*. This word, the Latin for 'it', was introduced for international use as the equivalent of the German 'Es' (originally used by Groddeck and adopted by Freud), because the conscious *ego*, the 'I' with which we are all familiar, often feels that the promptings arising from the unconscious are not part of itself, but come from something outside the conscious personality, something over which the conscious ego has no direct control. 'It', in fact, is putting pressure, sometimes irresistible pressure, on 'Me'. This 'external' pressure, when it was contrary to the conscious ego's standard of morality, was at one time, and sometimes still is, attributed to the Devil, or alternatively to an indwelling evil spirit. Of course the 'will' can restrict or refrain from actions suggested by these promptings, but it cannot prevent their arising.

Thus we conceive the mind as consisting not only of the conscious responsible ego in contact with the external world and shaped by the experience of life, but also of the uncon-scious id, to whose influences and promptings the ego is con-stantly exposed. Both ego and id are of course parts of the 'self' in a comprehensive sense.

This conception has a good deal in common with the fam-iliar picture of the morally responsible personality constantly struggling against the promptings of the 'lower nature', but the ethical setting is clearly inappropriate for psychological purposes. We must not forget that without our 'lower nature' we should have no earthly existence. It is just as much part of the self as the responsible ego, and biologically it is the prior part. Furthermore it is the source of human affection and very largely of creative art.

But there is another source of unconscious mental material which is the result of what is technically called *repression*, and it was the extensive existence of 'repressed' mental material and its profound effects in producing pathological symptoms that Freud originally discovered. It was this discovery that led to his conviction of the existence and importance of the unconscious mind, and then to the development of the technique and theory of psycho-analysis. Unlike the 'primary unconscious' or 'id' which is common to all humanity, the repressed material (which we may call the 'secondary unconscious') is the result of early experiences of the individual.

Much of the repressed unconscious material has at one time been conscious, or at least half-conscious, and has been repressed and forgotten, i.e. rendered unconscious, because it was repugnant to the conscious ego—unpleasant, acutely painful, or even horrifying, since it infringed, or even outraged, the ego's moral standards.[1] The material repressed very commonly relates to one of the two primary instincts—self preservation and sex—which we took as typical of the primary unconscious. Some, though certainly not all, of this repressed material comes into conflict with the moral standards of the ego—all of it is more or less acutely unpleasant to the ego— and is accordingly repressed as soon as it tends to reach the level of consciousness and seek overt expression. Just what material is admitted to consciousness and what rejected and repressed varies of course a great deal with the different characters and standards of different societies and different individuals, and is always dependent on early experience.

Very much of the repressed material is concerned with sex relations because these are the subject in many human societies of the most stringent moral codes whose infringement may involve the strongest feelings of guilt, or of shame and disgust, in the mind of the individual. Such feelings attach

---

[1] Some repressed material, however, has probably never at any time been *fully* conscious, but has always been, as it were, deliberately kept out of full consciousness. As Freud remarked it makes little difference whether you turn an unwelcome intruder out of your room and lock the door against him or whether you see him approach and lock the door before he can come in. Psychologically, as Franz Alexander says, repression is automatic, of the nature of a reflex inhibition, and presupposes an unconscious inner perception of the repugnant material.

most strongly to what are called 'abnormal' expressions of the sex instinct, notably, in our current western culture, incest, homosexuality and the so-called perversions of sex. There are many individuals who feel no particular guilt, shame or disgust in contemplating 'normal' sex relations, even those which transgress the current moral code, but shrink with the utmost repugnance from any suggestion of 'abnormal', or as it is often called 'unnatural' sex activity. Some people however, belonging to the well-known type of the extreme prude, have a horror, which can only be regarded as pathological, of everything connected with any kind of sex relationship. This horror sometimes leads to wholesale repression, though it may lead to fascinated and morbid absorption in the sexual affairs of other people, and in such cases the repressed instinct is finding a vicarious expression. These varieties of reaction are to be explained by the varying experiences, as well as by the psychological make-up of individuals; and it is the experiences of very early childhood that have the most profound and far-reaching effects in determining the attitudes of adult life and the varieties of reaction.

Repressed materials belonging to the instinct of self-preservation commonly arise from expressions of the instinct which are not 'permitted', are frowned upon by society, and tend to carry a feeling of guilt, though often not so poignant as that attaching to forbidden manifestations of sex. Such are physical cowardice on the one hand and especially extreme aggressiveness on the other. Both of these may arise from the instinct of self-preservation, but when this is exaggerated, to the extent for instance of the impulse to kill the object of aggression, it is likely to transgress the moral standards of the individual or to conflict with opposed impulses and thus to be repressed. Repression is always a sign of actual or at least of potential conflict between opposing impulses.

The fact that the contents of both the 'primary unconscious' (id) and of the 'secondary unconscious' (repressed mental material) relate mainly to the strongest primary instincts probably accounts for the initial failure to distinguish between them in spite of their totally different psychical origin and status, one being a universal primary constituent of the psychical organism, the other an accidental product, as it were, of the individual's particular development in relation to his particular environment.

What power or faculty of the mind is it that is able to repress these extremely strong primary instincts? The thoughts and impulses subject to repression are those which are painful or unpleasant, and also those which are not necessarily or even generally inherently unpleasant to human beings but are shocking or horrifying to the particular individual. The tendency to avoid, to shy away from, mental discomfort is universal and is due to the mind's continuous effort to escape disturbance of its equilibrium, but the specific avoidance of material which shocks the moral sense depends of course on the origin and nature of the moral sense of the particular individual.

It is clear that the moral sense begins to be built up in very early life—the newborn infant lacks it altogether—and that it is imposed on the developing self by the pressure of early experience acting through the people who make up the greatest part of the child's psychological environment. These of course are normally the parents, particularly the mother (or mother substitute) who is almost the whole of the infant's world during the first few weeks of life, on whom the child depends at first for its very existence, its comfort and well-being, and to whose standards it must conform as time goes on and its own ego develops under the inescapable pressure of the people who make up its world. These standards are at first impressed in the formation of physical habits and in the simpler aspects of behaviour: later on they include behaviour and conduct on a higher level, and the mother's influence is normally extended by the father's and later still by that of the school and other social agencies. In 'normal' development these cumulative influences gradually build up the child's own sense of right and wrong, laying the foundations of the *conscience* which guides its ethical reactions throughout life, as well as many reactions which do not reach the ethical level, such as the judgment of what is fitting and 'decent' in conduct as well as of what is ethically good or bad. The whole set of imperative influences affecting conduct, so far at least as they are at all consonant with the individual's own hereditary make-up, are thus absorbed into his mind and become the guides of his conduct. In the language of psycho-analysis these influences have been *introjected* into the developing mind and have become a permanent part of it. Together they form what Freud has called the *super-ego*, a dominant psychic 'instance'[1] throughout life and the effective cause of the repression of obnoxious material which is morally significant. The super-ego is largely though not wholly identical with the familiar 'conscience' and is closely connected with the 'ego-ideal', the half unconscious mental picture of the sort of person one would like, or ought, to be. This picture is often founded on the parental image—father or mother—or of some other dominant and admired personality[2] in the child's environment, but it may also of course be influenced or moulded by mental processes acting on general experience.

The super-ego, when once formed and active, thus shares with the id an effective influence on the responsible ego, and its normal working, like that of the id, is unconscious. Since the id represents the deep-lying instincts whose promptings often conflict with the demands of social life, and these social

[1] The German word *Instanz* is usefully applied to such a constant and powerful psychic influence, but its equivalent is not satisfactorily naturalized in the English language.

[2] When the child has come under criminal influences, either from parents or from associates older than itself, a criminal super-ego, derived from a perverted ego-ideal, e.g. the dominant leader of a gang of young ruffians, may be formed.

demands are commonly upheld by the super-ego (because the super-ego itself has taken origin from the precepts or examples of people whose own mental make-up has been moulded by the same social influences), there is inevitable conflict between the two. Freud draws a picture of the ego as the scene of these conflicts, strongly pushed in certain directions by the urgent instincts, threatened and bullied by the super-ego if it gives way to them. The conflicts may be perfectly conscious, and their sources clearly recognized; but very often they are not, for the influences that have formed the super-ego have penetrated deeply into the unconscious so that the ego does not understand the origin and nature of either of the forces which are disturbing its peace and harmony. The whole plexus of material involved is subject to repression, often because it is painful in its nature, and all the more when it is shocking to the moral sense and thus doubly painful.

It is such conflicts that psycho-analytic methods are specially well adapted to elucidate by bringing the unconscious material into full consciousness and thus enabling the conflict to be resolved in the light of reason and common sense. A heavy burden of unconscious guilt, directly caused by the action of the super-ego, is often revealed in the process and seen to be unjustified by a rational consideration of the case. The critical powers of the conscious ego are able to evaluate the forces that have been at work, both those of the id and those of the super-ego, and to make a fully conscious effort to establish harmony between them, withdrawing sanction from those, whether arising from the id or from the super-ego, which prove really incompatible with an integrated personality sufficiently adjusted to its actual environment. Even if some conflict remains, as it may well do, a full understanding of its nature and origin is enormously helpful in dealing with the troubles of actual life.

It is here that we can properly distinguish between the super-ego and the conscience. The super-ego and its actions are primarily unconscious and thus not subject to rational control. Some of its promptings may even be ethically bad. Conscience, when it embodies, as it should, fully conscious moral motives approved by the ego, represents the ethical side of the conscious self and has full moral authority. When we speak, in common talk, of an 'overscrupulous' or a 'tyrannical' conscience we are really criticizing the super-ego, and we should not allow the moral prestige of the idea of conscience to blind us to the fact that the super-ego is non-rational in origin, and that it often works positive and serious harm both to the individual and to those with whom he comes in contact. Conscience is a purified and rationalized super-ego, and when it is satisfactorily established the old unconscious super-ego tends to lose its separateness and to be merged in the ego.

To summarize the conceptual scheme of the human mind outlined in this chapter, we distinguish three levels of mental material in relation to consciousness, and three dominant psychical 'instances'. First there is the level of full consciousness, where mental processes take place in the sharp focus (or under the spotlight) of consciousness; secondly the level of the preconscious, containing material not in the spotlight but easily accessible to it; and thirdly the unconscious, not directly accessible to the spotlight. These levels are not sharply separated and material may pass from one to the other, in some cases easily, in others only with great difficulty. The three psychical 'instances' are first the ego in the narrower sense, the organ, as it were, of mental perception, conscious thought, judgment and will, in the closest relation with, and necessarily adapted to, the external world, that is to the particular set of conditions in which the individual lives; secondly the id, the spring of the instincts and affections, in closest relation with the living body and forming the essential vital basis of the self, on which its working is primarily unconscious; and thirdly the super-ego, superimposing a continuing

and largely unconscious influence on the ego, often conflicting with and checking the impulses coming from the id.

It must of course be realized and constantly kept in mind
that these conceptual constructions, like other scientific
concepts, are merely convenient machinery by means of
which we can group and deal with natural phenomena. In
some respects they are crude divisions of the immensely complicated set of functions which we call the mind. But the
justification of all such concepts lies in their usefulness, and
there is no doubt that these particular formulations have been
exceedingly helpful in disentangling the intricate complexities of mental process.

CHAPTER 3

THE ENERGY OF THE MIND

IN ORDER to get any sort of general mental picture of the
working of the human mind we have to postulate not only
mental or *psychic structure* but also *psychic energy* with which it
works. Psychic energy has not, of course, any close correlation with physical energy. Any given activity may mean the
expenditure of a great deal of physical, and very little psychic
energy, or vice versa. We may content ourselves here with
the old simple definition of energy as 'the power of doing
work', in this case psychic or mental work, and need not consider modern conceptions of the ultimate nature of physical
energy.

Mental structure is invisible and intangible and its constituents cannot be weighed or measured: the application of
the notion of structure to the mind is metaphorical. In the
same way we cannot measure mental or psychic energy,
though we have to *think* of it quantitatively. It is the power of
doing mental or psychic work and of bringing about changes
in the mind or psyche, just as changes in material things are
brought about through the action of physical energy. If we
start with the conception of physical energy, the application
of the term to psychic processes is metaphorical. But these
metaphors are indispensable to 'deep' psychology. We cannot form any satisfactory picture of the mind and its workings
without them.

We cannot postulate any principle of 'conservation' of psychic energy. Every individual mind has at its disposal a stock
of psychic energy which, like the physical energy of the living
body, disappears altogether, so far as we know, at death.
During an individual lifetime it is not constant in quantity
but increases with development and commonly decreases in

old age. It also constantly fluctuates during the course of life.

Psychic energy is most conspicuously seen in the working of the instincts and their derivatives—in self-preservation, in aggression, in play, in love and sex, and in all kinds of creative activity. It is also seen in 'pure' thought. Normally it has an outlet in action of one kind or another. When there is no such outlet an internal conflict of some kind preventing action is usually indicated.

There has been difference of opinion among psychologists as to the convertibility of psychic energy. Some hold that each of the various instincts which they recognize as primary, shows in its working a specific kind of energy, which is, so to speak, attached to that instinct, but that certain kinds can be more or less easily converted into other forms, for example sexual energy into the energy of artistic creation. The other view is that there is only one kind of universal psychic energy, the form it takes depending solely on the particular channel it uses, diversion from one channel to another varying in the ease with which it is accomplished. But the dispute is rather unreal, doubtfully more than verbal. At most it is merely a difference of view as to which of the two concepts is more useful in practice—and there is little to choose in this respect —but the second usage is the simpler and perhaps on the whole preferable.

Freud gave the name *libido* to the greater part of the psychic energy of an organism—ultimately, indeed, to the whole of what may be called 'life-promoting' energy—because he regarded it as essentially 'sexual', and this view is still orthodox among psycho-analysts: it is critically considered in Chapter 9. Jung at one time proposed to call *all* psychic energy 'libido', identifying it with psychic 'interest' and justifying this use by reference to historical examples; but he has not been generally followed. A very valuable conception of Freud's is the distinction between 'free libido' and 'fixed libido'. The state of 'occupation' (*Besetzung*) of a mental object by libido is now called *cathexis* (a keeping hold of), analogous to the 'locking up' of chemical energy (e.g. in a complex chemical molecule), or of 'atomic energy' in the nucleus of a chemical atom. When psychic energy 'sticks' in a mental object and is hard to dislodge it is said to be 'fixated'. Fixations of libido which occur in very early life (e.g. fixation on a parent) are particularly stubborn and are frequently contributory causes, if not indeed the primary causes, of serious mental trouble in later life.

Franz Alexander[1] has recently formulated three principles, largely based on Freud's work, concerned with the behaviour of psychic energy in the organism.

The first is the principle of *stability*, well known to physiologists, which dominates the organism in both physical and psychical spheres. This may be expressed as the tendency of living organisms to preserve the constancy of their internal conditions, and is well seen in the beautiful automatic mechanisms of warm-blooded animals which maintain the temperature of the body and the concentration of the body fluids, like blood and lymph, as nearly as possible at fixed levels—mechanisms which work on the general principle of a thermostat. The whole working economy of the bodies of the higher animals depends on the proper operation of this machinery. In the psychic sphere it is a function of the *ego* (in the sense defined in the last chapter) to maintain similar, even, internal conditions in the mind—though the psychic mechanisms do not work nearly so smoothly as the physical ones! The ego responds to every change in external or internal conditions which tends to disturb the equilibrium of the mind with its environment, striving to maintain harmonious conditions by altering one or the other.

The changes involved, and the appropriate responses, may be either physical or mental. *The organism, body and mind, works as a whole.* Thus if one suddenly feels a cold draught,

[1] *Fundamentals of Psychoanalysis*, George Allen and Unwin, London, 1948.

lowering the skin temperature and exposing one to the danger of a 'chill', one gets up and shuts the window or one moves one's seat. If one senses rising irritation in someone to whom one is talking one may change one's tone in an effort at appeasement, or in some circumstances, one may speak more sharply, in an effort to bring about a sudden change of attitude to the whole discussion, with a prospect of ultimate release of tension, occasionally realized! If one becomes aware of a strong internal urge to do something one either takes the appropriate action or, if that seems impossible, dangerous, or undesirable, one tries to suppress the desire, or to divert it into another channel, or to use the psychic energy aroused in some different way. All these actions are efforts to maintain or restore harmony between the organism and its environment and within the organism itself.

The ego senses the need of these adjustments through its powers of *perception*—external perception, through the senses, of hostile elements of the environment, and internal perception of disturbances in physico-chemical equilibrium, or of psychical need, or of mental conflict. It is able to effect adjustments through its *executive powers*, its control of the motor mechanisms of the body and also of a great part of the psychic machinery. These adjustments are largely unconscious—not only those directed to the maintenance of physico-chemical equilibrium—the need for rectification being satisfied unconsciously through the automatic physiological machinery of the 'autonomic' nervous system ('sympathetic' and 'parasympathetic'). Many of the psychical adjustments are also unconscious, though some of the needs for psychical adjustment rise into consciousness and are met by deliberate responses.

The whole picture is one of the maintenance of what is called *dynamic equilibrium*—a balance maintained, not in a state of complete repose, but by the interplay of forces, by constant small changes of adjustment to internal and external conditions. The living organism, body and mind together, is *par excellence* a system constantly kept as nearly as possible in dynamic equilibrium (see Chapter 7).

The second principle is that of *economy* in the use of energy. A child has to make constant *efforts* to acquire necessary physical and mental equipment—in learning to eat, to walk, to talk, to control its excretory functions, to behave in a manner which its family and other people will tolerate, and in countless minor ways: in the aggregate all this means the expenditure of a great deal of physical and mental energy. But many of these processes become, with constant practice, automatic: in other words *habits* are formed, which economize much of the energy that had to be spent in the process of learning. The same thing continues to happen throughout life when we learn new techniques of work or play, or when we establish routines which become automatic in performing our daily activities, so that we require a minimum of mental and physical energy to carry them out. The tendency to practise economy in the use of available energy is innate in the organism and is often given effect unconsciously.

But there is a danger to the organism when most of its activities have become automatic. Conditions change, new situations have to be confronted and the tendency is to deal with them in old-established ways which have been successful in the past in dealing with apparently similar situations, but which are not in fact well adapted to the new conditions. The organism tends to cling to automatic behaviour which was satisfactory in the past but is no longer adequate. To meet what are really novel situations flexible behaviour is required —and if they are urgent, sudden *ad hoc* responses and quick, almost unconscious, 'reasoning'.

One aspect of this danger where the psychic energy concerned is highly charged with emotion is seen in the 'fixation of libido' on an earlier love-object such as a parent, making it difficult or impossible to give love *freely* to a possible mate in adolescent or adult life. Initial emotions towards the new object are aroused, but the feelings tend to flow back into the old channels. These tendencies manifest themselves in various ways. Sometimes the sufferer from fixation finds it impossible to marry at all. In other instances the mate is expected to behave and react exactly like the father or mother, as the case may be, however different in character and temperament; in others again the victim of fixation unconsciously searches until he or she finds someone resembling the beloved parent as closely as possible. All this is usually done in complete ignorance of the psychical forces at work.

The general tendency to revert to an earlier pattern of behaviour when confronted with a novel, difficult or threatening situation was called by Freud *regression*. This is a universal human tendency, but is seen most conspicuously in neurotics and in 'weak' characters generally. Regression is economical of psychic energy, no doubt, but it is simply an automatic escape from the obligation to meet a new situation. The alert, vigorous mind, well adjusted to reality, flexible and used to dealing with changing conditions, rises to the occasion.

Alexander's third principle is that of *surplus energy*. During the growth and development of the child physical energy constantly increases, provided food supply is abundant and the general life conditions are good. With increasing size and complexity of the organism the field for storage and discharge of energy is rapidly enlarged, new and varied activities continually develop.

The supply of energy is in excess of the requirements of adaptation to the demands of existence in the protected life of the early years, and the surplus is discharged in all kinds of ways, notably in spontaneous *play*. Psychic energy in surplus develops in close relation to the physical, often appearing indeed as a direct concomitant—the healthy child is full of surplus vigour, both physical and mental, which *must* be discharged if the dynamic equilibrium of the organism is to be maintained. Physical activity is at first largely aimless movement and promiscuous play, but with the rapidly developing mind and increasing opportunities it gradually becomes canalized in purposeful play, and later in serious occupations. Alongside of this development come expressions of *love*, and also of *aggression*, towards other human beings and animals.

All these activities have an essential character in common: they are spontaneous expressions of surplus energy. They may all be called *erotic*, as Alexander suggests, if we widen the denotation of the word from its current narrow sexual meaning. In Plato, Eros is the god of all kinds of love. In the *Symposium* Phaedrus says that Love is the primeval god; after Chaos there were born these two, Earth and Love, but 'parents of Love there are none'; Eryximachus generalizes love as 'the attraction of all creatures to a great variety of things, working in the bodies of all animals, and all growths upon the earth'; Plato puts into the mouth of Diotima the view that Eros is not a god but a spirit (δαίμων). In the Athens of Plato the higher kind of love for human beings was homosexual, the love of men for boys, and in the *Symposium* Pausanias says that the meaner sort of man loves women as well as boys and is set on the body more than on the soul. Those inspired by the love that springs from the Heavenly goddess 'love boys only when they begin to acquire some mind'.

The older Greek god of Love, Eros, took the figure of a child whose activity was playful and spontaneous, 'mischievous' only in an innocent sense. In later Greek mythology Eros degenerated into the capricious god of sexual passion, the son of Zeus and Aphrodite, and the corresponding narrow use of the word 'erotic' is now almost universal.

In his play activities the child learns all sorts of aptitudes, physical and mental, which he can use later on in serious purposeful pursuits. In origin they serve for the discharge of surplus energy, eventually they are utilized as directed energy with definite willed ends. Organized games, and then professional game-playing, give transitions from spontaneous play to purposeful work, and there are many pursuits in which aptitudes acquired 'for fun' are used for serious purposes. In the sexual sphere the discharge of surplus energy serves equally for the spontaneous delights and ecstasies of love and for the continuation of the race. By the process of what is called 'sublimation' sexual energy, or, more correctly perhaps, energy which could easily and naturally find an outlet in sexual love, is used in creative art. The spontaneous drawing and painting of children, and a good deal of modern adult painting, too, is primarily an outlet for surplus psychic energy and follows paths which are not consciously directed, while the work of the accomplished adult artist is usually directed to definite ends and follows definite channels consciously conceived, though it should also retain the original element of spontaneity.

Alexander rightly insists that the only valid fundamental distinction in behaviour is between erotic (in the wide sense described, i.e. spontaneous) discharge of surplus energy, whatever its path, on the one hand, and purposeful integrated conduct on the other; but behaviour may be a blend of both, and the best creative work is precisely such a blend.

During development to adult life there is conflict between two tendencies in the human organism—the learning of new activities, originally for pleasure, for the sake of enjoyable outlets to surplus energy; and resistance to the progress towards maturity constantly seen in growing children and often leading to arrest or regression, the maintenance of old habits and ways of meeting situations, or the return to them from a more advanced stage of development which has not been firmly enough established. The refusal to grow up, typified in Barrie's Peter Pan, is quite common in children, and the retention of childish attitudes and behaviours is often enough seen in adults, quite apart from the serious pathological regressions of neurotics. Increasingly varied activity is a sign of the presence of surplus energy; refusal to engage in new activities is a sign that there is no energy to spare above what is being used in necessary or routine work. Both tendencies *in their proper place* help to maintain the stability of the dynamic system: outlets for surplus energy prevent the disturbance of the system's equilibrium by free unused energy, refusal to extend activity economizes energy which is wanted for use in established channels. On the political scene they are represented by the opposed 'progressive' and 'conservative' attitudes. Both are useful and indeed essential to health and balance of the organism, whether the individual or the state; either may be perverse or pathological.

It is noteworthy that the kind of psychology involved in this exposition is essentially based on the conception of *mechanism* and its working, the conception of psychic energy itself being derived from that of physical energy and the organism regarded as a physical 'system'. This is the point of view adopted by Freud which has been so fruitful in the development of 'deep psychology' during the past half century. The practical success of the concept of mechanism, not only in physical but in psychological science, is in fact undeniable. We must never forget, however, that in biology and psychology we are dealing with living organisms, and that while an organism *is* a machine it is also more than a machine.

CHAPTER 4

THE FUNCTIONS AND LIMITATIONS OF PSYCHOLOGICAL CONCEPTS

A CONCEPT is a general notion or idea formed in the mind and having a certain degree of definiteness. Very many concepts are definite ideas of *classes* of particular 'objects', using the word object in its widest sense as meaning any object of thought, and concepts of this kind, though they are not of course the only kind, form the simplest illustrations. Concepts furnish fixed points in thought, without which no abstract or systematic thinking of any kind would be possible, since the determination of the relations between different concepts is the basis of all systematic thought. Thus objects denoted by the concept of 'lion' are included among those denoted by the concept of 'animal', enabling us to say that all lions are animals but not all animals are lions. To take another example of widely different nature, the concept of love is the polar opposite of the concept of hate, yet both are included in the psychological concept of a *sentiment*. This means something different from the idea of 'sentiment' conveyed by the word in ordinary speech, where the meaning is imprecise and variable. But when we speak of 'sentiment' in ordinary speech and when we speak as psychologists of '*a* sentiment' (in the sense of McDougall) we mean, in both cases, some kind of 'affective' phenomenon of the human mind, i.e. a mental phenomenon involving emotion or 'feeling'. In other words the concept of an 'affective phenomenon' includes all ideas conveyed by the word 'sentiment', however used. We cannot think systematically about anything at all without using concepts at every step. Thus the basic function of a concept is to act as an instrument of orderly thought.

It is obvious that the formation of concepts dealing with

objects recognized through the senses is a very much more straightforward procedure than that involved in dealing with abstract ideas, emotions or mental processes. We are indeed forced by our mental make-up and the needs of everyday life to construct concepts concerning the objects around us. It is not a deliberate conscious process but happens imperceptibly as the result of observation and comparison and is necessary as a means of understanding and of enabling us to deal with our surroundings in the world. We *must* be able to separate the complex environment which confronts us into its elements, to compare like with like, and to give the same class-name to things which resemble one another more or less closely; and the giving of a name to such a collection of objects means that we have formed the concept of a class to which the objects belong.

So much for the formation of concepts in everyday life. The process must have begun even before incipient man acquired the power of speech, though it was certainly made very much easier when that power was attained and a name could be attached to each concept; but a rudimentary power of concept formation evidently exists at least in the anthropoids and in other higher animals.

In the sphere of science the process of concept formation is greatly extended and made much more precise. Scientific work requires the construction of concepts as exact as possible to form a basis for further observation and experiment, and hence the need for precise definition of the words representing scientific concepts, and for the invention of 'technical terms' when ordinary language does not contain words suitable for the purpose. An example of this need was amusingly illustrated a few years ago when an eminent public man complained in *The Times* of the scientific jargon unnecessarily employed in the use of the term 'dehydrated' instead of 'dry'. It had to be pointed out that 'dehydration' means the abstraction of all the free water that *can* be abstracted from a given substance, while 'drying' is an imprecise and purely relative term.

The history of thought as well as current literature, especially of course newspaper writing, abounds in examples of confused and misleading arguments founded on the use of ambiguous words taken from current language and capable of different interpretations by different people. The greatest possible precision in concept formation and definition is indispensable to valid scientific or philosophical argument. That does not mean however that imprecise or even erroneous concepts never have any value. The history of scientific theory is largely a history of the gradual improvement of concepts, which were at first often vague and were sometimes found to be invalid and useless, as knowledge of the relevant material increased. Some scientific concepts, such as that of 'phlogiston' in chemistry and (much later) of the 'ether' in physics, have had to be discarded when the facts on which they were based were more thoroughly explored. Others have had their content profoundly modified as a result of new discoveries, though the concept may still relate to the same things. Thus the chemical atom was at one time thought to be the smallest possible form of matter—'uncuttable' as its name implies—and perfectly homogeneous, but it is now held to have a complex internal structure which can be disintegrated. Yet it is the same atom, though, according to modern physics, an entity of very different nature from that of Dalton's concept. These earlier concepts represented steps in the progress of science, some of them, at least, essential steps. A most important function of scientific concepts is to render possible the formulation of hypotheses in which they are used, and this is an indispensable process in the advance of science. With the progress of knowledge many hypotheses have to be discarded, and very often the concepts employed in the hypothesis are shown to be invalid. Nevertheless they have served a useful purpose because they have been stepping stones to completer knowledge.

In philosophy, by universal consent the most difficult subject of human thought, we find that every original philosopher made concepts of his own and often described them in language which was unintelligible to the plain man, as well as being at variance with those of most other philosophers. One of the latest schools of philosophy, that of 'logical analysis', claims to show that practically the whole of metaphysics, traditionally the very core of philosophy, has no intelligible relation to any sort of reality, since the phrases and arguments of metaphysicians do not make sense when translated into language intelligible to the plain man, and their conclusions cannot be verified. Yet few would deny that the work of philosophers, from the Greeks onwards, has immensely enriched human thought. William James said that philosophy was only a specially determined attempt to think clearly. And though the efforts of the metaphysicians to think clearly may have been constantly frustrated they have certainly added enormously to our intellectual and spiritual possessions. Yet metaphysics is compact of varying concepts the validity of which is quite unverifiable.

When we turn to the concepts of psychology we are compelled to draw a distinction between 'laboratory psychology', from Wundt's work in the mid-nineteenth century to the products of innumerable American laboratories in the present day, and the so-called 'deep psychology' of psycho-analysis and allied schools. Much of the former is very closely connected with the physiology of the special senses, though the laboratory results are related more to mental than to physiological function. But the mental functions studied in the laboratory are relatively superficial functions of the mind though they are those through which we carry out our everyday mental and physical work and a thorough analysis of them is of great practical importance. The concepts employed are of the same general type as those of other branches of science. This kind of work aims at *quantitative* results obtained through *measurement* of human reactions to various stimuli.

In the fields of general and 'deep' psychology, on the other hand, where we try to analyse and determine the relations of mental processes which from their nature cannot be measured the procedure is quite different. Here we cannot at once isolate a particular type of reaction to stimulus but have to take the human mind as a whole into account and do our best to interpret and clarify its bewilderingly interwoven and often unexpected reactions. Our objects of study are complex human personalities, no longer material objects or isolable processes, and psychology is unique among the sciences, as Franz Alexander points out, in that *the object observed is a being similar to the observer*. This at once gives us, indeed forces upon us, a method of investigation totally different from those of the natural sciences (which deal with material objects and physical processes), a method based upon what psycho-analysts call *identification*. We interpret the movements, the facial expressions, the tones of voice and the contents of speech of others through our knowledge of what goes on in our own minds when we act and speak similarly—introspection and comparison are indispensable means of research. In its crude form this is simply the method we all use in carrying on our ordinary relationships with our fellow-men every day of our lives. This 'common sense' knowledge of other human beings is of course often unreliable as we sometimes find out to our cost in ordinary life, just as the immediate interpretation of crude visual observation may turn out to be partly or even wholly illusory. It often requires to be refined, checked, and extended by continuous research just as visual observation is refined and extended with the help of various physical instruments such as the telescope and the microscope.

'Deep psychology', as its name implies, is concerned with the 'depths' of the mind and its concepts are necessarily difficult to formulate with confidence. It is impossible to *observe* the 'depths' of other people's minds, or even of our own mind, directly, and we can rarely study them experimentally, while 'controlled' experiment is out of the question. All we can observe is what comes into consciousness and we can only observe what comes into our own consciousness. Even that is difficult enough. The very conception of the existence of mental 'depths' is an inference from conscious experience, and all the psycho-analytic concepts—the unconscious, libido, cathexis, the id, the super-ego, etc.—are concepts constructed to explain and correlate certain phenomena of consciousness and behaviour and are used to form elaborate theories of the nature and working of the 'mind as a whole' in the sense described in Chapters 1 and 2.

Though the method of investigation is so different, the justification of these concepts rests on exactly the same ultimate grounds as those of the concepts of the various branches of physical and biological science, namely their usefulness in enabling us to understand the phenomena which we observe. One can no more dispense with appropriate concepts in deep psychology than one can dispense with the concepts of common sense in daily life, or with those of the various branches of natural science in the study of the different subjects. But the indirectness of the access to consciousness of the mental processes involved and the fact that they are subject to strong emotional influences to which ordinary scientific thinking is not, or at any rate is much less, subject, combined with the inherent obscurity and elusiveness of the material, makes the formation and manipulation of the concepts concerned a difficult and delicate task. According to Freudian theory the workings of the unconscious mind are of an entirely different nature from those with which we are familiar in consciousness, and this we must accept if we are to use psycho-analysis at all. Language was developed to apply first to the objects of the external world, and then to our conscious feelings. It is not to be expected that it will easily be successfully applied to the obscure workings of the unconscious mind. We may often get on the track of something real which is nevertheless extremely difficult to name and characterize. Consequently we must expect the concepts of 'deep psychology' to be peculiarly vulnerable to criticism, and the divergences that exist between different 'schools' are not at all surprising. We cannot and must not expect the universal agreement and acceptance to which we are accustomed in the well-established concepts of physical science.

The success of Freud in formulating concepts which have established their usefulness and enabled 'orthodox' psychoanalysis to develop a more or less coherent body of viable theory is primarily due to his remarkable psychological insight, constructive imagination, and persistent refusal to be deflected from his own lines of thought and work in the face of bitter opposition and contemptuous ridicule. It would be strange indeed if Freud had not made mistakes and if every one of his concepts escaped damaging criticism.[1] It would also be strange if none of the formulations of other talented workers in the field of 'deep psychology', not belonging to Freud's school, could find a place in the theory of the subject.

The question remains: are we to consider 'deep psychology' as a branch of science? In the present writer's view the answer is decidedly that we must, in spite of the essential difference in mode of approach, and for the reason already indicated, that many of the concepts of psycho-analysis are actually useful, and at present indispensable, in successful attempts to understand the mental processes underlying much of human conscious experience and behaviour, just as the concepts of chemistry, physics and biology are indispensable for the understanding of the world of physical energy and of living beings. The method of psycho-analytic research inaugurated by Freud is in this respect the regular method of all scientific research—observation, comparison, the formulation of concepts by abstraction and then of hypotheses based upon them,

[1] Some such criticisms are suggested in Chapter 9.

followed by further observation and comparison for the purpose of verification or disproof. It is true that experiment, the most potent instrument in the familiar branches of science, cannot be used extensively in psycho-analysis, and controlled experiment not at all, and this is a severe handicap. The only possible method of verification of psycho-analytic hypotheses is further observation and comparison. The validity of postulated psychical mechanisms can only be tested by repeated applications to successive cases and the various psychical processes at work thus gradually sifted out. It has been found that the same reactions to the same or similar situations constantly recur, and many of the concepts formed to resume them have ultimately justified themselves by fitting the psychical facts over a wider and wider range of experience. They are found to apply also to everyday psychical phenomena and to explain behaviour quite remote from that of the neurotic patients with whom Freud was at first exclusively concerned. For these reasons psycho-analysis has a perfectly good claim to be a valid part of the science of the human mind. But it is a very difficult science, and for the reasons given we should expect many mistakes to be made, false paths pursued, and untenable theses put forward. It is essential to keep a perfectly open mind in regard to the validity of some of its current tenets, though others we cannot avoid accepting as well established and forming the necessary basis of further research in what has certainly been a most fruitful field of study.

CHAPTER 5

INSTINCT, HEREDITY AND ENVIRONMENT

THE CONCEPTION of instinct is a key concept in modern psychology, one which we cannot do without, though there has recently been a strong tendency on the part of many writers (largely following a fashionable trend of thought which we shall have occasion to criticize) to minimize or even to deny the value of the conception as applied to human beings. During the last forty years there has been a good deal of rather confused controversy about instinct, mainly due, it would seem, to misapprehension of the facts and of their proper application to human psychology.

Much of this controversy dated from the publication in 1908 of McDougall's *Introduction to Social Psychology*. McDougall used the conception of instinct as the basis of his important work and described instincts as 'innate special tendencies of the mind that are common to all members of any one species, racial characters that have been slowly evolved in the process of adaptation of species to their environment and that can be neither eradicated from the mental constitution of which they are innate elements nor acquired by individuals in the course of their lifetime'. He further defined an instinct as 'an inherited or innate psycho-physical disposition which determines its possessor to perceive, and to pay attention, to objects of a certain class, to experience an emotional excitement of a particular quality upon perceiving such an object, and to act in regard to it in a particular manner, or at least to experience an impulse to such action'. He then went on to distinguish twelve[1] separate 'simple instincts' which he held could be recognized in the human being, and proceeded to

[1] Later extended to fourteen: see footnote on p. 52.

describe each and to show how their various combinations in the human mind build up a number of more or less stable mental structures, which, largely following Shand, he called the *sentiments*. With these permanent structures of the *individual* mind which determine its attitude and therefore its behaviour in the various situations it may encounter we are not here immediately concerned. But the nature and validity of the instinct mechanisms which lie at their roots are of basic importance.

For examples we may take two of McDougall's 'simple' instincts whose *primary* working is particularly straightforward and which are essential to the survival of the individual and the species. There is the instinct to seek food so as to satisfy hunger by eating; and there is the instinct of lust or sexual attraction[1] to a desirable member of the opposite sex, and its satisfaction in the act of mating. In each of these there is an initial recognition of the object which excites the instinct, the resulting emotion or 'affect', and the appropriate impulse to action.

McDougall's book had an immense influence on the subsequent course of psychological thinking. On one hand it was used as the basis of further investigation and analysis, and on the other it was attacked on various grounds, which were partly well founded but partly untenable. The main lines of attack were two. It was said that McDougall's use of the conception of separate instincts as the determining forces of human behaviour hypostatized various aspects of behaviour, creating a number of what have been called 'occult entities' (compare the 'occult qualities' of Aristotle) which merely replaced the discredited mental 'faculties' at one time supposed to represent the springs of human activity, and, like the 'faculties', served to divert attention from the need for fundamental analysis of the causes and conditions of be-

[1] McDougall originally masked this well-defined primary instinct under the name of the instinct of reproduction. See Chapter 8.

haviour. It was also said that the conception of instinct might be valid in considering the reactions of animals to their environment, but that the behaviour of human beings was so completely governed by tradition, education, and the particular social milieu—now usually known collectively as a 'culture'—in which they grew up that the effects of any remains of 'instincts' inherited from animal ancestors were practically negligible. The first criticism had, as we shall see, some, though not complete, justification.

The second accords with the modern tendency to exalt the importance of environment and to 'play down' the influence of heredity in human life; and it often allies itself (though it is not of course identical) with the modern insistence on the primacy of the human community in which the individual lives and to which his interests must be subordinated—an insistence that finds its extreme expression in the thesis that the individual exists to serve the State, in opposition to the old 'liberal' thesis that the State exists to promote the welfare and happiness of the individual. In this circle of ideas human beings are thought of as roughly equivalent units that can be moulded by education, by the pressure of 'public opinion' (which may even be created by the State authority through calculated and persistent propaganda) and by the pressure of the law, into any form desired by the State authority. Their individual differences may be safely ignored where they cannot be used for State purposes, and the existing diversities of type between the populations of different countries are held to be entirely the results of their different histories and of the different forms of pressure that have been exerted upon them. In reality, according to this school of thought, they all consist of more or less uniform human material, and what can be done to one can be done to all if the appropriate means are employed.

Before we can hope to arrive at anything like a true picture of the factors involved in human behaviour, it is essential to try to distinguish the truth from the falsehood in these views.

The view that the instincts are unimportant in determining human behaviour is flatly opposed to the evidence of the biological evolution of the human race from anthropoid ancestors, whose modern representatives[1] show instinctive reactions which have much in common and are sometimes identical with human behaviour in similar situations. It is true of course that in man an immense mental superstructure has been erected, and new values have appeared which in many respects transcend and may even contradict 'instinctive values'. In the pursuit of these 'higher values' a man may act in ways directly contrary to those which would lead to the straightforward satisfaction of his instincts. It is also true that the human environment in which he grows up plays a very large part in moulding his behaviour. It is the weight of these last facts that has led to the mistaken denial of instincts as the *foundations* of man's behaviour, however bewildering the complexities that have been built upon them. For example, Julian Huxley has written that 'man differs from all other organisms in having at his disposal no complex pattern of instinctive behaviour for dealing with the problems with which existence confronts him'. It is perfectly true that the machinery of instinctive patterns is far more sharply marked and closely circumscribed and the mode of its working much less variable in particular species of animal than in man. But it is also true that the instincts are present and basically effective in man, though there is much more flexibility in their mode of action because of his much more complex mind and the enormous weight of his cultural environment.

By McDougall's definition instincts are 'common to all the members of any one species', and the basic human instincts

---

[1] The sub-human ancestors of man were not, according to modern work, closely allied to the stock of the existing anthropoid apes, but the latter certainly show many of the same 'human' characters, presumably by parallel evolution.

are shared by human races of the most diverse character, environment, tradition and mode of life, by the inhabitants of the United States no less than by those of New Guinea, by the French colonists of North Africa or Indo-China no less than by the Esquimaux of Greenland. It is this underlying uniformity of instinct in the human species which gives an apparent justification to the theory that national *character*, the sum of the features in which one nation differs from another, is wholly dependent upon the 'culture' of a particular tribe or nation. In fact both the culture and the national or tribal character are alike the product of heredity *plus* environment, as are all the characters of living organisms.

Then there is the further theory, fashionable in some circles, that the State (which means of course the governing authorities of the State) can produce any desired change in the mentality of any population by using the appropriate means. A great deal of 'moulding' can no doubt be done in this way, but it is quite extravagant to suppose that such efforts can be uniformly successful. Some peoples are obstinately resistant to pressure of the kind, and if their resistance is unsuccessful they may dwindle and ultimately disappear rather than change in the desired direction.

All human beings agree in their general type of bodily structure, in the physiological mechanisms associated with it, and in the instinctive equipment which basically determines their mental and physical reactions in the situations they all encounter. These are hereditary characters common to all members of the human species. But it is obvious that in both physical and mental features different human beings also show wide differences, and that many of these are also hereditary, depending on their particular parentage and ancestry, though some are greatly influenced by the conditions in which they they live. A man not only inherits the colour of his skin and his bodily framework from his parents or grandparents, but also his talent for music or for scientific research, as well as many features of his emotional disposition. The detailed course of this individual heredity can often be followed out in human families, and it can be studied more exactly in the controlled breeding of plants and animals. The aggregation of people which we call a tribe or nation shows many such differences among the individuals of which it is composed, but it also shows features, both mental and physical, which, if not common to all, are at least common to a majority of the population; and it is these which form the foundation of what is called 'national character'.[1] On this foundation the national character is built, moulded of course to a very important degree by the history and traditions of the particular tribe or nation and by the physical and social environment in which the population exists.

The basic features of national character are thus handed down from generation to generation, partly by the physical mechanism of biological heredity and partly by tradition— sometimes called 'social heredity'; and the differences between the characters of different nations, or between different segregated races living in the same country, are obvious enough.

Few would deny that this is true as between the native

[1] In 1940 Mr Hamilton Fyfe published a book called *The Illusion of National Character* in which he set out to show that no such thing as national character exists. The book is full of fallacious argument ostensibly based on a number of facts that are actually quite irrelevant; and the conclusions are reached by emphasizing the fundamental resemblances between nations which flow from the fact that they all consist of human beings and that many are prone to change their attitudes and much of their behaviour, sometimes very quickly, under the influence of strong common emotions, often stimulated by interested propaganda. No one doubts these resemblances, but the well-marked lasting differences which the ordinary man quite reasonably calls national character are simply ignored by Mr Fyfe. The enthusiastic praise of the book by H. G. Wells, Bernard Shaw, Norman Angell and C. E. M. Joad was clearly due to the wishful thinking of these eminent writers, all of whom, though widely different in personality, are or were idealistic internationalists and liked to believe that serious obstacles to the realization of their ideals were non-existent or could at least be minimized.

Bantu peoples and the white inhabitants of South Africa, or between American Indians and the peoples of European origin who have occupied and dominated the American continent. But when we come to the peoples of the different European countries, for example, who resemble one another much more closely, it has become fashionable to attribute their differences solely to their different cultures, to their various geographical environments, their different histories and the different national traditions which have been built up in the course of centuries. There can be no question that geography, history, tradition, and characteristic culture have had an enormous influence in creating national character as we see it today; but it is equally true that hereditary factors have had a great part in its production and are in fact the basic material on which the environmental factors work.

The differences of physical appearance *and* of behaviour between a crowd of South Europeans and a crowd of Dutchmen or Swedes will scarcely be denied, and certainly cannot be attributed *entirely* to history or tradition. We cannot divorce hereditary types of physique from hereditary types of mentality, for there is plenty of evidence that they are often closely correlated. Even among the different nations of southern or of northern Europe there are physical, and, it is safe to assert, correlated mental differences which are inherited. In spite of the relatively close kinship of the English and the Germans there is a German (and more particularly a Prussian) type of physique and mentality that is distinctly different from the English, and certainly has a hereditary foundation. The divergent national mentalities have been fostered and developed, but not created, by divergent histories.

It is not of course contended that these national characteristics are found in every member of a population. In the first place there is great variety of physical and mental type in each nation, and there are many Scandinavians, Dutchmen, Germans, northern Frenchmen, and even northern Italians, who do not greatly differ in physique and appearance, or in mental make-up, from many Englishmen. Those who contend that the characteristics of a modern western nation depend entirely on its history, traditions and 'social atmosphere' are concerned to combat the absurd theories of extreme 'racialism' which assume that the people of a modern nation all belong to a single racial stock (mixed of course with a certain number of 'aliens'). It is quite rightly pointed out that the populations of western Europe are in fact largely mongrels of very mixed heredity derived from different original stocks. If one makes the assumption opposite to that of the racialists and supposes that this mixing has been universal and complete, so that the human material is substantially uniform throughout Europe, the conclusion that national character depends entirely on history and environment would logically follow, for there would be no other possible causes. But geographical and political barriers, economic factors, conditions of life, and emotional prejudices have always prevented anything like free migration and inter-marriage between the members of different nations and even between those of different ways of life in one nation, with the result that local segregation of certain types of physique and character has occurred, partly more or less coincident with national boundaries and partly within individual nations.[1] Superposed on these partly mixed and partly segregated masses of people, historical causes—social, political, economic, military and religious—have finally produced the characters of the different nations as we know them today. And the prevailing innate qualities of any given nation or of any given local population within a nation have also played a large part in determining the effects of these environ-

[1] A similar segregation, the result of barriers of different kinds separating different parts of a population of plants or animals, representing different hereditary 'strains' but originally belonging to one species, has been one of the most important factors in the differentiation of new species derived from an original one.

mental factors on its character. Different dominant types of mental make-up react differently to particular external pressures.

Among a certain school of modern anthropologists, of whom Margaret Mead is a good example, the views just expressed have become very unfashionable. In her book on *The American Character* (Pelican Books 1944)[1] she asserts, 'on the basis of modern anthropological findings', that 'it is not blood but upbringing that determines all of these ways of behaving' among 'people potentially similar at birth'; and again, 'as new-born babies we (Americans) didn't differ from German babies or Japanese babies or English babies or Russian babies . . . all of us, culturally speaking, were *tabula rasa*'.

Some of these statements are ambiguous and their total effect is most misleading. It is obviously true that new-born babies are *tabula rasa* 'culturally speaking', because they have not begun to be affected by the culture in which they will be brought up, but it is quite ridiculous to say that American, German, Japanese, English and Russian babies 'do not differ'. People are no doubt potentially *similar* at birth since they are all human beings, but that is not to say they 'do not differ' as aggregates (populations or nations), just as they do as individuals, in hereditary characters. Does Margaret Mead seriously believe that the Pilgrim Fathers as a group were not a selected fraction of the English nation, carrying to New England qualities of character and temperament not shared by all their fellow-countrymen? Of course they brought with them the Puritan tradition and ideals, but they also brought the innate qualities which adhered to and could sustain those traditions. Why did they or their forbears *become* Puritans, as some Englishmen did and others did not? To say that 'modern anthropological findings' have established that 'it is not blood but upbringing that determines ways of behaving' is simply not true. It is 'blood' *plus* 'upbringing', and adult character and behaviour are the

[1] Originally published in America in 1942 as *Keep Your Powder Dry*.

results of a subtle blending of the two. Anthropology cannot by any available methods distinguish accurately between hereditary psychological characters and those acquired as a result of upbringing. It might conceivably be done by transplanting sets of new-born babies from one national environment to another, but really conclusive experiments on such lines would meet with almost insuperable difficulties!

Julian Huxley, though he is primarily a biologist, is not unaffected by the modern tendency to 'play down' heredity, though he evidently has some qualms about it. In reviewing Margaret Mead's latest book (*Male and Female*, 1949) he writes: 'Even if it should prove that genetic differences of temperament between races and between the sexes in different races play some rôle in determining the behaviour of men and women we can be sure that this is quite subsidiary to the effects of what they learn through the cultural pattern into which they are born'. But you cannot treat genetic (i.e. hereditary) factors and environmental factors as if they were causes of similar nature and say that one is subsidiary to the other. It is comparable to saying that the steel of which a bridge is built is 'subsidiary' in the final result to the construction. You can only say that a particular feature of the resulting bridge is due to the steel or due to the construction *if you are able to separate the lines of causation*, and this cannot be effectively done, at any rate at present, with many features of human behaviour. Or to take a biological parallel, an oak tree growing in particular conditions of soil, illumination and exposure to wind takes on a particular form of trunk and branch development. These are said to be due to the environmental factors acting upon it as it grows up, but *the particular form of response* is due to the tree's hereditary characters as an oak and is different from that of any other kind of tree exposed to the same conditions. In all cases both heredity and environment are certainly involved.

When we turn from the nations of Europe to the new

nations developed across the Atlantic we find very special conditions of development. The people of the United States
present a particularly interesting field for the consideration
of these problems, for their origin and history are unique in a
very real sense. To the various societies formed by the original
colonists—and though these belonged to different European
nations in different parts of the sub-continent it was mainly
those of English stock who first came to the east coast that
determined the dominant American culture which has ultimately emerged. The enormous immigrations of the nineteenth and the beginning of the twentieth century added
representatives of almost all the continental European countries, adventuring in a new transatlantic life or fleeing from
the tyranny of their homelands. In this way there was provided a great variety of human hereditary material as the basis
of the modern American nation.

One of the dominant factors in the development of American culture was the necessity of constant struggle with a rich
but often hostile environment. A great subcontinent was there
to be explored, exploited and subdued to human needs and
desires, a magnificent field for the stimulation and employment of every kind of adventurous energy. The result, as
we all know, has been the creation, by the middle of the
twentieth century, of the wealthiest and most powerful nation
in the world, and at the same time the establishment of a
lasting tradition of successful individual effort. Success, primarily material success, the creation and amassing of wealth,
became the almost universal aim of the healthy American
adolescent, and the degree of success attained became the
standard by which all were judged and estimated to a far
greater degree than in the complex and relatively static societies of Europe. The masses of immigrants from these European societies were rapidly assimilated, in two or three generations, to this American type. They forgot their native
languages and the customs of their original homelands and

joined in the American struggle for individual betterment, but they contributed richly by their varied talents and temperaments to the development of American civilization. The impress of their European culture disappeared to all intents and purposes in their immediate descendants, but the hereditary characters of their racial origin did not. The permanent contributions of Mediterranean immigrants were not identical with those of Central European or with those of Scandinavians, and the marked differences between them are still evident enough in particular areas of the United States which were populated almost entirely by immigrants of a particular race. These differences were certainly not created solely by the different cultures of the nations independently of hereditary differences. The original national cultures of these communities have in fact largely vanished in their descendants, but not the hereditary physical and mental characters. Hereditary differences make the development of varied cultures possible in the first instance, but it is the hereditary foundation which is permanent and physically transmitted. The elements of culture fluctuate with changes in external conditions and the character of a culture alters and may disappear.

Alongside the constant striving for material success a moral factor was also of prime importance. The moral traditions of the sixteenth and seventeenth century Puritan colonists became another dominant factor in the development of American culture and, as in Britain itself, the Puritan type of religion was fitted harmoniously into the struggle for material success. Together with abundant energy and the willingness to take risks, a relatively ascetic life, a strict sexual code and the practice of honesty and good faith in business affairs were very favourable conditions for the successful achievement of wealth. The successful man, at least on these lines, was obviously approved by the Almighty, who showed His approval by granting the success. Thus the successful struggle was supported and sanctioned by the confident assurance of right-eousness.

The opportunities of acquiring great wealth are now much more restricted than they were in the latter half of the nine-teenth century, when they were open to almost anyone with the right talents and abundant energy. But the urge to climb the social ladder by making more and more money remains a vital motive in what may be called the American 'middle classes' to which a great proportion of the population belongs. Increase of wealth means rise in social status, which is ex-pressed by the style of the home and its furniture, ownership of the right kind of automobile, the clothes of the wife, and so on.

Thus the current American civilization has had a wonder-fully wide foundation of varied hereditary endowments drawn from nearly the whole of Europe but all governed by the constant striving for material advancement and at the same time an underlying faith in righteousness and a need for the approval of the Almighty. It is true enough that sinister ele-ments—corruption, crooked dealings, gangsterism and vio-lent crime—have also been conspicuously present, but it must be remembered that the 'news value' of such things is very great, so that they have had a publicity out of all proportion to the place they have actually occupied in American life. Such scandals are 'splashed' in the newspaper headlines, but they also arouse a demand for the fullest investigation and and punishment of the offenders. The underlying fundamental morality of the American people is an essential national character.

In considering hereditary factors in the determination of national character we must of course, as already indicated, distinguish between individual heredity, the physical and men-tal features transmitted from individual parents to offspring, and heredity as it appears in whole populations. The latter is of course nothing but the aggregate effect of all the individual cases, but it is a phenomenon which we may, and indeed must, consider separately when we are dealing with the character of a nation as a whole. The common inheritance of certain characters of body and mind in large numbers of a population, the existence of well-marked *types* of physique and mentality which are represented widely enough to exercise a preponderant influence on the population as a whole, is of crucial importance in determining national character. It is the basic element on which the manifold effects of environment play and which they mould into shapes characteristic of the nation.

It is in fact quite as futile to try to explain the characters of human communities as it is to explain those of individual organisms without taking into account *both* heredity *and* environment—both nature and nurture. Every biological organism and every population of organisms is equipped with a certain stock of hereditary determinants ('genes') which are identifiable material substances, and on this stock its possibilities of development depend. In any large population the available stock of genes is of course immensely greater and more varied than in any single individual belonging to it. In the course of development of the individual the genes and their products act upon one another, and the developing organism reacts also to the particular conditions to which it is exposed. Development in fact essentially depends on the constant interplay between genetic and environmental factors. The same is true of the 'super-organism' represented by any particular human community, only here the results are far more complex and include the results of the mixing of different stocks in the community and those profound effects of daily life in a community and of public opinion upon individuals, which we called the social environment in its widest sense.

If we then start with the postulate that instincts, in the

sense defined, form the basis of human behaviour, we must return to the first criticism of McDougall's work, which was that his 'simple instincts' were hypostatizations of groups of psycho-physical processes, creating what have been called 'occult' entities or qualities like the old 'faculties', and diverting attention from fundamental analysis of these processes. This criticism has some justification but is not entirely fair. McDougall's conception and its detailed working-out represented a great advance on the theory of 'faculties' and on the older treatments of instinct, because it dealt in detail with the *nature* of an instinct and with the relation of its working to those of other instincts and to other elements of the human mind. It does not hinder a fresh analysis of his 'simple instincts', either on the physiological or the psychological side. But what can fairly be said is that McDougall's enumeration of twelve (or fourteen) simple instincts[1] tended to create a misleading impression of definiteness and finality, as if they were comparable, for example, with the chemical elements of the periodic table. Furthermore a specific affect or emotion to which a definite name can be given was not easily assigned to all of the different 'simple instincts' enumerated by McDougall, as is shown by his original failure to find an appropriate affect for several of them, and by the unsatisfactoriness of the names given to some of those affects which he did assign. Several critics doubted whether the accompaniment of a specific emotion was always a character-

---

[1] McDougall's original list was as follows: flight (fear), pugnacity (anger), repulsion (disgust), curiosity (wonder), self-assertion (elation or positive self-feeling), self-abasement (subjection or negative self-feeling), parental instinct (tenderness), reproduction, feeding, gregariousness, acquisition, construction. The words in parenthesis are the emotions supposed to accompany the activities of each instinct. In his *Energies of Man*, published in 1945, McDougall added the instincts (or, as he now called them, 'propensities') of *appeal* and *laughter* to the list: he also changed the titles of some, and named the specific affects (for which he had not originally found names) supposed to be attached to the last five in the above list. It is very doubtful if these changes were real improvements on the original exposition.

istic of a specific instinct, though some of them are obvious enough.

The activities of the mind are in fact so complicated and interwoven that a classification of this sort cannot be ultimately valid. Different writers on the subject have recognized very different lists of instincts, while Freud, in the end, reduced them to two—the 'life' and 'death' instincts—a conception we shall have occasion to criticize in a later chapter. This sort of disagreement, if it persists, is nearly always a sign that an impossible task is being attempted because the problem has not been properly posed, and we may fairly conclude that the most fruitful psychological analysis cannot aim at a precise classification of instincts, but must concern itself rather with analysis of particular psychical *processes*.

That does not mean, however, that the concept of instinct is of no value. McDougall's great service consisted in bringing out very clearly the nature of the instinct *mechanism*, and the fact that at least a large part of elementary psychical activity is primarily based upon it. If we abandon the attempt to make an exhaustive list of instincts, we may still give the name of instinct to chains of psychical processes which are clearly of the same general type without supposing that we have reached any sort of finality in analysis. There are innate mental processes of this sort which are relatively simple, and others which are not simple, but which nevertheless do involve McDougall's three characteristics: (1) specific perception of, and attention to, something in the environment or in the mind itself, (2) often the experience of a more or less specific emotion aroused by that something, and (3) the urge to take action in regard to it.

It may be objected that this description is too wide and would include mental processes that no one would call instinctive; but if we retain, as we must, McDougall's proviso that an instinct is common to all the members of a species and is therefore hereditary throughout the species the concept

c

has great value because it characterizes a fundamental phenomenon of human psychology. Then we can usefully recognize
certain innate dispositions (or propensities) of the human
mind which are of this nature, which underlie the infinite
complexities of human behaviour, and to which we can give
the name of instinct, without in any way binding ourselves to
a fixed list of such dispositions. Some of these, as has been
said, are relatively simple, closely bound up with specific
physiological processes, such for example as the hunger and
sex instincts; others are quite complex. Among these others
are the 'herd instinct', an extension of McDougall's 'gregarious instinct', and described in detail by Wilfred Trotter in
his well-known book[1]; and perhaps also the 'religious instinct', not recognized by McDougall as a simple instinct. We
must certainly agree that each of these is complex, built up
from pre-existing simpler elements, but both have the essential features of the instinct mechanism.

Thus the herd instinct is based on the specific sensitiveness
of the individual mind of the gregarious animal to suggestions
arising from the herd to which it belongs. The normal individual is driven to obey these suggestions: if he does not do so he
is miserable, or at least uncomfortable, if he does he experiences a specific satisfaction because he feels that he is at one
with his herd. Many of the suggestions or laws of the herd are
traditionally voiced by a 'herd leader'—king, chief, president,
or other prominent figure in any given herd, or they are determined by a governing herd council, but most are conveyed
by the contacts of everyday life. The herd instinct no doubt
takes origin in the individual life from association of the young
child with his family, in which the father (or mother) naturally corresponds to the 'herd leader', while the 'family
council' corresponds to the herd assembly. But the consolidated herd instinct of the adult shows all the characteristics of
McDougall's definition of instinct.

[1] *Instincts of the Herd in Peace and War* (1916).

The status of religion as based on a 'religious instinct' is much more doubtful, largely because we cannot confidently assert the universality of such an instinct in the human species. In its developed form it conforms pretty closely to the definition of an instinct. The individual recognizes the existence of something outside himself, and greater than himself, to which something inside himself responds. Both of these he calls 'spirit', and in most of the great modern religions the 'outside something' is typically identified with a supreme God. The impulse of the individual is to worship the supreme God, and when he gives his mind to worship his feeling of spiritual satisfaction is quite specific.

But is this attitude universal in the human race? Certainly not in this developed form. From our knowledge of history and of contemporary forms of religion among primitive tribes we can make plausible conjectures as to the way in which it was gradually built up. McDougall would construct the typical religious attitude of *reverence* from several of his simple emotions attached to his simple instincts—fear, wonder, subjection (negative self-feeling) and tender emotion. But however it was built up historically, or in the individual mind of the contemporary Christian, the religious attitude certainly possesses, in its developed form, most of the characteristics of an instinct. Here it is the constituent elements (rather than the developed mechanism) which are inherited. Another reason for doubt is that many modern men would deny that they possess any religious tendencies. Who shall say whether this is true, or whether they are repressing mental content, which they dislike or are afraid of, into the unconscious?

We may conclude that the conception of instinct is inescapable—that it represents a psychical reality basically actuating human behaviour, but that we cannot compile a final and satisfactory 'list' of instincts. Rather we have to recognize a *type* of linked perception, feeling, and behaviour which we call 'instinctive', which is common to the human race, and to which in many cases we can give an appropriate specific name. In the human race behaviour actuated by the instincts is far more flexible and modifiable than in animals other than man, but the now fashionable denial of the reality of instincts as fundamental motives of human feeling and behaviour cannot be sustained.

CHAPTER 6

CAUSATION, DETERMINISM
AND FREE WILL

THE CONTROVERSY about free will and determinism is a
very old one, and innumerable books and essays have been
written on the subject. Stated in the crudest terms it is a conflict between the belief that all the phenomena of nature, including those of the human mind, are connected by chains of
'causation' according to determined sequences which can
sometimes be accurately ascertained and generalized as 'natural laws'[1] and on the other hand the belief that some occurrences at least are the results of the intervention of the 'will',
either of supernatural agencies, as in the case of 'miracles'
(often thought of as the direct result of the will of God leading to a departure from the normal order of nature), or of the
human will, which chooses between alternatives apparently
unconstrained by any inexorable sequence of psychical processes within the mind of the chooser. But there have been
some thinkers who have contended that there is no contra-
diction between the theory of universal determinism and a
belief in human free will interpreted in any sense that can be
valid.

First of all it is necessary to consider just what we we mean
by cause and causation, concepts which have themselves
undergone some modification and led to much discussion,
especially in recent times. To the plain man there is no difficulty. He pushes a spade into the earth and throws out the
soil, repeating the action till a hole is dug. His digging is the
cause, the hole is the effect. Someone is infected with the
germs of a serious disease, develops its known symptoms,

[1] This is the meaning of determinism employed throughout this chapter;
but there is a different sense in which it is used by many physicists; see p. 59.

and dies. The germs are the cause, his illness and death the effects.

But when we look a little deeper we realize that we cannot always *generalize* the statements about the effects of these 'causes', for they do not always lead to the same results: other factors are involved in the observed sequences. In some soils it is difficult or impossible to dig a hole with a spade. The digger may dig, but a hole does not result. Another man may develop the same disease and recover. A third man is altogether immune from the disease: the bacteria have no effect upon him. The nature of the soil and the constitution of the person attacked are also 'causes' or, if we like, necessary 'conditions' of the events, the distinction between causes and conditions being largely artificial. We must therefore conclude that particular events depend upon many causes which co-operate to produce the observed effect; or, in other words, that causation is always multiple. But for convenience we may often pick out a conspicuous determining action, such as the work of the man digging or the action of the germs which have entered the other man's body as the 'active' cause—we may even call it *the* cause (sometimes spoken of as the '*causa causans*') of the hole or of the death, relegating to the status of 'conditions' the other elements necessary to the result.

In the study of multiple causation the determination by mathematical methods of correlation of the causes or conditions necessary to the occurrence of certain results in large numbers of cases is now possible in 'advanced' branches of science, and has led to the disuse in all such work of the old simple concept of cause and effect. This procedure has become the rule wherever large bodies of data can be accurately observed and treated mathematically so that general 'laws' can be stated in mathematical terms. This can be done in many departments of physics and chemistry and increasingly in those branches of biology and sociology where great numbers of cases can be recorded quantitatively from observation or controlled experiment and mathematical treatment applied.

In all such work a principal aim is to be able to *predict* the outcome of given sets of events and conditions. Predictability is recognized as the mark of exact science, but it can only be realized within limits. There is always a margin of error that cannot be eliminated—the prediction is true, within narrow limits, of a large number of events taken as a whole. The quantitative results of separate observations of the same phenomenon differ to a greater or less extent—in statistical language they show a 'scatter' which follows the 'laws of chance'.

The interest in the power of prediction and its great practical importance have led physicists to think of, and even to define 'determinism' in terms of predictability. Thus Professor Max Born writes that 'determinism postulates that events at different times are connected by laws in such a way that predictions of unknown situations (past or future) can be made'.[1] This of course is a different meaning from that given at the beginning of the chapter, which expresses a belief that all phenomena are connected by chains of causation; and this last is the sense in which the word determinism is used in our present discussion. The difference between the two definitions partly accounts for the refusal of many mathematical physicists to subscribe to the doctrine of determinism. In point of fact observation never determines the *exact* values of physical quantities, but this fact need not hinder the belief that they *have* exact values, even though these can never be *precisely* determined by observation and analysis. There is always a margin of error.

The points can be conveniently illustrated by the procedure of life insurance statisticians who predict, on the basis of the records ('vital statistics'), the *probable* length of life of insured persons. The predictions are so accurate on the whole, when all the insured people are taken together, that an insur-

[1] *Natural Philosophy of Cause and Chance* (1949), p. 9.

ance company is certain, within narrow limits, of making the calculated rate of profit on the aggregate of the insurance policies of the large group. Prediction can, of course, also be made of the length of life of any individual person, but here the prediction would often be wildly wrong since the margin of error is much greater, so great in fact that his life could not be safely insured unless the lives of a great many other people were being insured at the same time: the risk of serious loss would be too large, though there would be an equal *possibility* of a large profit. With a great number of individuals insured at the same time both these possibilities are very much reduced. While some die prematurely when they have paid very few premiums, so that the company loses money on them, others live beyond the probable age and the company makes more profit on their policies than that which would accrue at the calculated rate. But these opposite cases balance one another, or 'average out', over the whole number of insured persons, and there is a very close approximation to the predicted result of the aggregate transaction. The length of life predicted as probable cannot be true of each individual person insured because the causes which determine the actual date of death of an individual are so many and various that the cleverest doctor could not forecast it with any accuracy.

Exactly the same principle holds for all scientific work which deals mathematically with large numbers of individual cases. Predictions are often so true within very narrow limits that they can be formulated as 'laws of nature', but they are not necessarily true of individual events which cannot be dealt with separately. In modern atomic or 'electronic' physics, the development of which has proceeded from certain very fruitful initial hypotheses about the internal structure of atoms, this is conspicuously the case. The physicist deals with vast numbers of atoms which, in the light of these hypotheses, can be broken up experimentally into their 'electronic' constituents, but the motions of individual electrons or other infra-atomic particles cannot be determined or predicted, since all electrons are identical in nature and the only way to detect them is by means of other electrons. Thus any statement about the positions and movements of one particular specified electron is, at least in the present state of science, essentially meaningless. The physicist can say nothing about it—he has no means of doing so—just as the actuary can say nothing about the date of the death of a particular insured person, of whose existence, as an individual, he has in fact no knowledge. These conditions justify such statements as Eddington's—'The physicist may or may not believe in determinism, but in his own domain he has at present no evidence for it and, what is more, he has at present no use for it'. In other words physicists predict to a high degree of probability on a statistical basis and this procedure does not use the concept of determinism.

But besides the impossibility of dealing with individual electrons because they cannot be individually known there are other fundamental reasons why the laws of causation applicable to objects which can be directly perceived cannot be applied to the behaviour of atoms and infra-atomic particles. These also depend partly on their smallness, and they are well described in Martin Johnson's *Science and the Meanings of Truth* (1946).

Causation in the sphere of large-scale physics (mechanics) essentially depends on the relation of inertia to acceleration discovered by Newton and explained in his law of gravitation. This law was successfully applied to the movements of the planets of our solar system and to all macroscopic objects on the earth's surface. In the nineteenth century mechanical laws were successfully used to explain the behaviour of the masses of moving molecules, of which gases are composed, at different temperatures and pressures (dynamic theory of gases), though such molecules are submicroscopic and cannot be directly perceived.

But when we come down to the atoms into which molecules may break up, and to the protons, electrons and other
infra-atomic particles, of which, according to modern physics, atoms are composed, and which are said to be of the
order of a million million times smaller than atoms, the principles of mechanics no longer hold. One reason for this is
because 'the ultimate connection between observer and observed is in principle the locating of the latter by the pattern
of the radiation he scatters (as in the ordinary perception by
the eye of illuminated macroscopic objects and, with the aid
of the microscope, of sub-macroscopic—i.e. microscopic—
objects). For all objects whose size is large compared with
the wavelength of the light or other available radiation
linking observer with observed this locating can be achieved
without altering any specification in the physical description
of the object. But the smaller the object the more the process of radiation-scattering modifies the very quantity we set
out to observe. In fact, of the pair of data required for
mechanical prediction—position and velocity—the closer
the one is approached as a definable quantity the more elusive
the other becomes in the growing latitude it imposes on our
error of measurement. In the end the process of "knowing"
destroys the "known" ' (Johnson, *op. cit.*, p. 42). Thus the
velocity of an electron at a known position cannot even be
physically defined, so that in atomic physics causal *definition*
is intrinsically impossible. This was pointed out by Heisenberg and formulated as the 'Principle of Indeterminacy'.

Perhaps the most fundamental hindrance to defining causation in the behaviour of these excessively minute entities is
the 'interpenetration' of the mutually exclusive categories of
inertia or mass and momentum or energy on which the
fundamental concept of mechanism essentially depends. 'The
inertia or mass of the smallest bodies, typically the electron
capable of the highest speeds, increases measurably with
velocities of extreme magnitude.' Again, 'radiation possesses

an inertia of its own—the mass and therefore the momentum of radiation is quantitatively detectable' (*op. cit.*, p. 33). An example of this radical 'interpenetration' of concepts is the 'ascription of wave properties to electrons and other particles, and of particle properties to radiation (formerly considered an essentially wave phenomenon) . . . all constituents of matter can be profitably treated in some of their character as non-material wave phenomena . . . (and) some of the properties of a beam of light . . . have become intelligible by treating the beam as a hail of particles . . . such particles are not to be regarded as material but as localized regions of high energy content' (p. 34). Thus 'the constituents of matter and the facts of radiation both vacillate disconcertingly between the two behaviours of wave and particle, each of which has a mechanical meaning, but a meaning each exclusive of the other'. Both are derived from large-scale observation of perceptible things which exemplify Newtonian mechanics. 'For an electron to "be" a wave and also to "be" a particle deprives either description of that decisiveness which was the essence of passing from hypothesis to law . . .' (p. 35).

The writings of atomic physicists have led to a strong attack on determinism as a fundamental principle of nature. Eddington points out that since all physical phenomena involve the 'indeterminate'[1] motions of electrons there is everywhere an element of indeterminacy, though this is small in large-scale phenomena concerned with the motions of relatively large bodies, where the effects of mass are more important than the movements of electrons. On this ground Heisenberg's 'uncertainty principle', according to which the precise behaviour of an electron cannot be predicted, even in principle, is made into a fundamental principle of the universe. On the lines of this thesis it has even been argued that in the psychical sphere, 'free will', in the sense of freedom from the constraint of definite sequences of phenomena, may exist.

[1] In the sense that they cannot be precisely 'determined' by observation.

But individual occurrences that can be investigated separately do not fall within the sphere of these considerations, which are irrelevant to them, and in the case of such individual occurrences as can be observed and studied the old concept of cause and effect is inescapable, every effect or event being determined by multiple causes or conditions. If I hit a billiard ball with a cue and the ball runs over the table in a straight line and hits another ball so that it also moves, we are compelled to think of my action in striking the first ball as the *determining cause* of its rectilinear motion (strictly as the 'active' or conspicuous determining cause) and the motion of the second ball as *caused*, i.e. *determined*, by the impact of the first; though here also, as in the instances of digging the hole and of the fatal disease, other conditions or causes are necessary to the event—a spherical ball hit squarely at a particular spot, a level and even 'cloth', and so on.

And there is a further point. The act of hitting the ball is *voluntary*; it has been preceded by a definite intention formed in the mind of the striker and the work of a number of his muscles has been co-ordinated to that particular end. In other words there are mental events preceding and determining the physical act of striking the ball, and these particular mental events are preceded and determined by others, such as forming the intention to play billiards. Thus we have psychical and physical events following and passing into one another in causal chains—a network of lines of causation which join and branch and join again perpetually. Each event, represented by a point of junction of the lines, is determined by many causes together, and each event in its turn determines further causal sequences, represented by branches from the point corresponding with the event.

This of course is a schematic picture of the familiar flow of events in the phenomenal world, any one of which we may mentally isolate from the flux of happenings so as to fix our attention on its causes and consequences. In this way we are led to the postulate of universal determinism—that no event is uncaused—a postulate so necessary for the conduct of practical affairs and the pursuit of elementary science that both in science and in everyday life it is just taken for granted.

Apart from miracles (and even a divine miracle, though it interrupts the 'order of nature' as we understand it, is *caused* by the will of God and may properly be considered as part of His 'higher order') no one questions the universality of determinism in the physical world: at least no one did question it until the extraordinary red herring—in itself a perfectly good herring—of the 'uncertainty principle' was drawn across the philosophical path. This, as we have seen, depends partly on a special kind of scientific procedure adapted to the analysis of large numbers of events where knowledge of individual events is unobtainable, and in particular to analysis of the ultimate constitution of matter and energy where the units involved are excessively minute and ordinary mechanical principles do not apply; but this has no relation to the causal analysis of an individual event. When you cannot obtain knowledge of individual events the principle of indeterminacy holds—you cannot make predictions about them—but that is a totally different thing from believing that such events are uncaused, from denying the principle of universal determinism in nature. The word determinism in fact is being used in two different senses—the first relating to causation, the second to predictability. All our experience goes to show that nature is orderly, and this order seems to involve an acceptance of universal determinism in the first sense. The assumption of the existence of uncaused events not only contradicts the orderliness which has always been revealed wherever it has been sought with adequate means of investigation, but appears in itself as a kind of monstrosity which it is difficult, if not impossible, to picture in terms of external reality. An uncaused event would be an event quite isolated from other events, and of such isolation we have no experience.

We must, of course, be careful not to think of causation as a kind of mysterious *force* giving rise to sequences of phenomena. It is simply an expression of the fact that regular sequences are found to exist wherever we have been able to investigate them—in other words that nature is orderly, not chaotic.

In the psychical sphere there is often difficulty in establishing causal sequences, partly because of the elusiveness of psychical phenomena and the obscurity attaching to many of them. The only *direct* means of observing them is introspection, and the carrying out of objective analysis by introspection is beset by obstacles that do not usually affect the observation and analysis of external nature. But we know that mental processes are often in fact determined by one another—so much is quite clear from introspection alone—and the question remains whether causal determination is not as valid throughout the psychical as it is throughout the physical sphere. The case for such a belief has been immensely strengthened through the discovery of a method by which we can at least partially evade the customary difficulties of introspection, and through the recognition of the reality and nature of an unconscious part of the mind which determines many of our thoughts and actions as well as the greatest part of our feelings and affections. The method of psycho-analysis and the recognition of the unconscious have greatly widened the sphere within which we can establish sequences of causation within the mind and in the transitions between mental processes and external actions, many of which are at first sight extremely obscure.

But there has always been and there still is a strong human intuition of the 'freedom of the will' and we have to consider first whether this intuition is wholly illusory, and, if not, in what sense it may be valid; secondly, if it is not illusory, whether a real freedom of the will does or does not contradict the universal validity of determinism in the psychic sphere. Before we can discuss these questions we must be clear as to what we mean by *will*.

Will implies something more than wish or desire. These may come into consciousness momentarily, disappearing immediately as the result of satisfaction, or of the acceptance of the impossibility of satisfaction, or of replacement by some stronger impulse. Will, on the other hand, at least in the sense here employed, is a stable disposition of the mind definitely related to a complex of circumstances and defining the mind's attitude towards them. It is always and necessarily based on the needs of the mind as a whole, but it is something more than the sum of isolated reactions to individual needs: it is an integrated quasi-permanent disposition of the mind essentially concerned with *action*. The execution of will may demand a series of complicated actions directed to a goal that may be more or less remote. People who are capable of continuous effort towards the ends to which their wills are directed, who come back again and again, in spite of recurring frustrations, to the courses of action which they believe will lead to their goals, are said to be strong-willed: those who are easily turned aside from the pursuit have weak or unstable wills.

That is will in the most comprehensive sense, but 'freedom of the will' is also applied to particular limited choices not necessarily integrated into extensive courses of action directed to more or less remote goals. We now have to ask whether human wills are determined by antecedent factors, and in what sense, if any, they can properly be considered 'free'.

There is, as we have seen, a strong general case for universal psychical as well as physical determinism, and this is based on recognition of the unity of the organism and the close interdependence of body and mind, as well as on our greatly increased knowledge of psychical causation. We may in fact argue that an uncaused psychical event is as anomalous and as difficult to conceive as an uncaused physical event. From such a standpoint it is easy to contend that the intuition of human freedom is necessarily illusory, that (since all his thoughts and actions are determined by precedent causes) the individual is never really free to choose, though he may think that he is.

Such a view has been strenuously attacked in the interests of the moral order. If a man is constrained to a wrong course of action by an inescapable causal sequence how can he be blamed for pursuing it? Belief in universal determinism in the psychical sphere would seem to be subversive of individual moral responsibility as well as to contradict the persistent belief in the freedom of the human will. Can we reconcile these opposites? I believe they can be reconciled through a consideration of the nature and complexity of the human mind.

As we have seen in Chapter 5 there is a great deal of good evidence that the mind of the individual human being is built upon a basis of instincts, and the mechanisms of many are inherited from sub-human ancestors. In Chapter 5 we saw reason to deprecate a fashionable tendency to deny or underrate the fundamental importance of instincts. But with civilized man's enormously increased mental equipment and under the influence of his powerful and immensely complex environment the *expressions* of these basic urges often undergo profound changes, though the underlying instincts which are the ultimate motive forces of his behaviour can be recognized on analysis. The conflicts between the three mental institutions which were described in Chapter 2—the *id* (instinctive foundation), the *ego* (adult conscious personality more or less closely adapted to its particular environment), and the *super-ego* (an introjected authority transformed into 'conscience' in the morally responsible person)—complicate thought, feeling, and behaviour still further.

Let us consider first a well-endowed, well-balanced, highly

civilized individual who would be regarded by the society
in which he lives as a morally responsible 'man of good
will'. Such a person would have a well-integrated ego,
suitably adapted to the circumstances of his life, able to direct
the id impulses into appropriate channels, and a super-ego
which was not tyrannous but had been transformed into a rational though sufficiently sensitive conscience. In making difficult decisions involving action he would often have to weigh
pros and cons with great care, but in doing so he would
undoubtedly be influenced, whether he realized it or not, by
a great many impulses and prejudices, arising from his own
nature and temperament and given form within his mind by
his experience of life in his own society. Whether he arrived
at a conclusion on objective grounds and thus gave his rational
faculty its proper function, or whether he 'rationalized' his
impulses and prejudices, providing a false façade of 'reason'
for his decision, he would feel and know that the processes
leading to that decision were *his own* mental processes. They
belonged to him alone; they were part of him. The fact that
they were all determined by antecedent factors, whether he
recognized these factors or not, would not diminish that cer-
tainty in the least degree, for the antecedent factors all took
origin within, or had passed through the selective sieve of his
own mind. His decisions would be the free decisions of his
own personality and he would rightly be sure that the ensuing
actions were the results of his own free will. He was acting
in accordance with his own nature and was not constrained by
any direct external pressure. That is the only sense in which a
human being's will can be free. The suggestion that freedom
of the will means something other than this, that it involves
some mysterious mental process independent of antecedent
factors, is entirely illusory, as alien from the whole of our
knowledge and experience as an uncaused physical event.

Consciousness of possible alternative choices is the basis
of the feeling of freedom. There are two or more possible

courses of action because there is more than one motive involved, and many concomitant conditions. The line of least
resistance *when all are taken into consideration* is the line that
will be followed, but it is often impossible to say beforehand
what that line will be.

It need hardly be said that we are not all as well-integrated
and well-balanced as the individual whose mental workings
we have been considering. In arriving at decisions or taking
action many of us are largely swayed by prejudice or passion,
and we may react immediately and violently to an external
situation without any attempt to allow reason to perform its
regulating function. In such cases a man is often said to be
'a victim to prejudice', 'the slave of his passions' or 'a creature of impulse'. These psychical forces are then thought of
in the same way that external compulsion is thought of, as
something independent of the man's 'real self'; or, when we
have to admit that his passions are an important part of his
'real self', independent of his 'better self', which is regarded
in some sense as the core of his being. It is a case of the 'it'
putting pressure on the 'me'. The man is not, and often does
not feel, completely free, because an important part of his
psychical motivations are not under central control.

We conclude then that freedom of the will is a function of
the integration of the personality, that the more completely
a man's psychic processes are harmonised and knit together
the freer he is, and the freer he feels, in thought and in
action. This feeling is in no sense an illusion, though every
one of his thoughts and actions is determined by antecedent
factors.

And these considerations answer the contention that the
assertion of universal determinism destroys moral responsibility. We judge the man as a whole, as an integrated being,
and we condemn him morally if his passions are out of central
control, leading to actions which transgress the moral code of
his society or his individual moral code. The responsibility

of the man is to maintain a course of integrated conduct in which conscience and reason play a determining part. These are the internal regulating factors which are expected to come into play. If they do not he is to that extent a moral failure and, as such, is condemned.

Normally the introjected super-ego which forms the foundation of the conscience is so shaped as to be in line with the accepted moral code of the community, but where it is weak or defective owing to the weakness or absence of the parental influences to which it ordinarily owes its origin through the establishment of a super-ego, the dictates of the normal conscience may be replaced by a very different code, learned from later associates. It is this which is probably seen in the gangsterism of adolescents, where a perverted and sometimes very strict code of behaviour associated with systematic criminality is adopted in accordance with herd instinct from the 'partial herd' represented by the gang to which the adolescent belongs. This perverted 'gang conscience' may be very well adapted to the immediate conditions and interests of this partial herd, while it directly contravenes the normal type of conscience prevailing in the community at large, which has been developed through the generations in accordance with the permanent interests—or what are thought to be the permanent interests—of that particular society, and embodies the recognized 'social virtues'.

It may be said, of course, that if a man is a moral failure he cannot always help it. His wrong conduct may be determined by overwhelming antecedent causes—heredity or external circumstances or both—for which he is not responsible. That may well be true in a number of cases, and such people require pity and help, or, in extreme cases, restraint. They are in a position similar to that of sufferers from physical or mental disability or disease caused by heredity or external circumstances, or both. But there is this difference. Normally there is at least the foundation of a conscience, derived from the super-ego, which can be developed and given an opportunity to determine conduct, and the consciousness of this provides a weapon not open to the man who is physically or mentally ill. No doubt there are people who have no conscience that can be made effective; they are to be found in a certain type of criminal and nothing but forcible restraint is indicated. There is no possibility of freedom here. The internal compulsions to wrong conduct have to be answered by external compulsion. But that is not true of most of us, in whom, given the formation of a super-ego, conscience is a normal and necessary element of the psychic equipment. Psychical integration, central control, on which freedom of the will essentially depends, cannot be acquired without it.

CHAPTER 7

TELEOLOGY, EQUILIBRIUM AND DYNAMIC SYSTEMS

IN THE last two chapters we have considered some of the motivations of human behaviour and have seen reason to believe that behaviour is determined by regular sequences of mental and physical events which we call causation, discussed in the last chapter. A very large part of this behaviour is ordered by the pursuit of *ends*, conscious or unconscious, and is called *teleological* (Greek τέλος, an end accomplished, the completion or fulfilment of anything). This pursuit can be shown to follow the universal law of the *tendency* towards the attainment of *equilibrium* or balance, which is characteristic of the sequences of all phenomena of which we have knowledge, whether physical or psychical. The various forces which bring about change in any local aggregation of matter continue to act until the distribution of energy is such that no further change is possible under the given conditions, or at least the changes have become so slow that the configuration of the aggregate and the amount and nature of its total energy changes are not perceptibly altered within an appropriate period of observation, which is, of course, very different in different cases. Then we recognize an entity which we may call a physical *system*. In such a system the constituent elements (matter and energy) are in a state of approximate balance. In very various physical spheres, and notably in the living organism, the sequences of change result in establishment of systems in what is called *dynamic equilibrium*, i.e. the forces at work within the system, and between the system and its surroundings are continually bringing about changes; but these changes are continuously compensated by other changes, so that the configuration of the system and the gen-

eral distribution of energy within it remain for a longer or
shorter time approximately constant. Such a dynamic equilibrium is, however, apparently always more or less imperfect
and precarious, so that the system is fated eventually to break
up and disappear. Such a system is also of course very often
destroyed by the impact of external forces, either before or
after it has attained approximate equilibrium, but many persist
for long periods of time. In the present chapter it is proposed
to attempt an analysis of these conceptions and to examine
their relationships.

Human activities involving chains of causation which are
thought of as leading to, or aiming at, definite ends or goals,
when considered from the standpoint of those ends are said
to be teleological. Thus if I decide to make a particular piece
of apparatus or to give a lecture on a particular topic, of
which I have a defined idea, to establish a new organization, or
to win a particular woman in marriage, my thoughts and
actions are adapted to achieving that definite *purpose*. They
form a continuous chain of causation, at first mental and then
translated into action, a *directed* chain, given significance as a
whole by the end to be attained. While each event is determined by the preceding ones the whole series is determined
by the end in view. This end is then said to be the 'final' or
teleological cause of all the events, while the 'efficient' cause
of each lies in a physical or mental process or processes preceding it in the sequence. It is clear that in any conscious and
purposive human activity the end is first conceived as an idea
in the mind which is consciously active throughout the whole
process except where the necessary successive actions, once
the series is started, have become automatic through constant
practice. The universe is sometimes described as an idea in
the mind of God, and then the orderly processes of nature
become parts of His universal scheme leading to a consummation at which we can only guess. That is an all-embracing
teleology; but every teleological action, great or small, by

a conscious being, is purposive, and we know of 'purpose' (in the strict sense) only in the mind of a conscious being.

Human purposes are by no means always conscious. The preliminary psychical processes leading to primary instinctive actions begin, as we have seen, in the unconscious, though the later stages, in the human being at least, rise to full consciousness. And the purposes of actions arising from one of the numerous bypaths taken by instincts which have been modified or distorted as a result of the action of the super-ego or the pressure of the environment may be refused recognition and repressed altogether because the conscious personality is ashamed of the purpose and cannot admit to himself the end to which his actions are leading. Psycho-analytic case histories are full of examples of such refusals.

There is, however, another kind of teleology which does not involve mental purpose. Living organisms consist of structures and are the fields of processes which promote their living activity and are often indeed essential to their continued existence. At one time these were attributed to the direct work of the Almighty, forming parts of His design for the living creation: with the acceptance of the theory of organic evolution it became generally believed by biologists that these useful structures and processes have been gradually developed as a result of the operation of natural selection. In the struggle for existence those organisms which developed heritable characters establishing efficient and harmonious internal working, as well as characters adapted to deal with the external environment, were enabled to survive in particular conditions of life and in competition with other organisms, and thus to transmit the adaptive characters to their offspring. These adaptations to internal and external life may extend to every kind of quality and character that an organism can possess—gross and minute structure of the body as a whole and of all its organs, physiological processes of every sort; in the higher animals mental characters too, particularly the so-

called instincts which are of prime importance to survival;
and finally the capacity for acquiring the flexible skills and
the general intelligence and power of reasoning which have
led to the overwhelming dominance of the human race.

These 'adaptive' characters are often said to 'serve a purpose', but the meaning here is clearly different from that of
the 'purposes' which are formed in the human mind and is
only used by analogy. Human purposes may have useful ends
but they may also have harmful or destructive ones. Their
distinctive character is the mental formulation of a typical
conscious end to which action is directed, though as we have
seen we also have to recognize *unconscious* purpose in the
human mind. The only common quality of a human purpose
and the 'purpose' or 'function' of an 'adaptive character' of
an organism is that both can be considered or 'interpreted'
teleologically—that is in relation to an end—in the first case
a consciously formulated or unconsciously existent mental
goal which is realized or attempted in action, in the second
case the development through natural selection of some character which helps to adjust the species to its mode of life.

When the theory of organic evolution by natural selection
was more and more widely accepted in the latter part of the
nineteenth century it so captured the imagination of biologists that there was a widespread effort to find a 'use'—an
adaptation—in every detail of the structures of animals and
plants. Many of these efforts were quite successful, but there
were also put forward far-fetched 'interpretations' of various
structures for whose adaptive value there was no sufficient
evidence from observation or experiment, the interpretation
resting only on the unsupported speculation of the observer.
In several cases it was ultimately shown by closer observation
and by experiment that the structures concerned could not
have the functions attributed to them.

This uncontrolled speculation led to a strong reaction
among biologists and a tendency to discredit all 'teleological'

interpretation. It was freely argued that the only sound line of biological research was investigation of the physico-chemical causation, i.e. of the 'efficient causes', of biological phenomena, irrespective of whether they are or are not 'useful' to the organism. It was also contended that in order to establish a good case for the origin of a character through the action of natural selection it was always necessary to prove that it was not only 'useful' to its possessor but that it actually possessed a 'survival value', or in other words that its presence was crucial in the struggle for existence, that it actually made the difference between life and death before the breeding period—and the point was often very difficult or apparently impossible to determine.

There can be no question that this reaction was on the whole a healthy one, and the great advances in physiological and biochemical science which marked the turn of the century and have continued ever since have led to a very considerable widening and deepening of our knowledge of the mechanisms of vital processes.

But there was another important development of biological research which also began at the turn of the century and which eventually placed the process of natural selection in a new light. This was the rediscovery of Mendel's work on heredity, which had been carried out several decades earlier but had remained unknown to biologists largely because it had been published in an obscure journal. Mendel's experiments were repeated and the laws of inheritance which he discovered were confirmed. As the result of these events, work on biological heredity was immensely stimulated and a most fruitful new branch of biology, called *genetics*, was developed. A new theory of the mechanism of heredity was formulated and the existence of well-defined units or *genes*, situated in the cell nuclei and carrying hereditary characters from parent to offspring, was established. Since the nature and interrelationships of the genes carried by parents are the basic

factors in determining the structures and specific constitutions of the offspring, it is clear that the genetic make-up
(genotype) of particular parents selected for breeding determines both the bodily constitution (phenotype) and also the
genotype of the next generation. The interactions of co-
existing genes in the course of individual development were
shown, as the new century advanced, to be complicated and
subtle, so that slight changes in the selection of breeding
parents, by altering gene relationships, may have far-reaching,
though often gradual, effects in successive generations.

It thus became clear that the scope of the action of natural
selection is much more delicate and searching than was understood in the nineteenth century. The study of heredity was
brought within the sphere of biochemical investigation, and
the artificial antagonism between the physico-chemical and
the teleological standpoints tended to disappear. The development of 'useful' characters, not only adaptations to external environment but gradual complication and co-ordination between internal processes which build up an increasing
efficiency of the organism's economy, is now seen as a gradual
series of transformations based on physico-chemical changes
and controlled by natural selection through the selection and
transmission of particular genes.

All such developmental processes may be brought under
the concept of increasing approach to *equilibrium*, which is a
general law of the physical world and is applicable, as has
been said, to all long-term processes of every kind of which
we have knowledge—psychological, social, economic and
political as well as biological, chemical and physical.

The most familiar type of equilibrium is, of course, that in
which the state of equilibrium appears to be a state of rest, as
when a boulder rolls down a slope and comes to rest at the
bottom, or when a chemical reaction results in the formation
of stable chemical compounds which remain intact until some
more powerful chemical or physical agency breaks up the co-

herence of the atoms in the stable molecules. This kind of equilibrium may be called *static*, though we must remember that the continuously acting opposed forces of gravity and the resistance of the earth upon which the boulder rests are effective in keeping it in its new position, and that it is the forces of interatomic cohesion in the stable molecules which keep the chemical substance intact. In contrast we have the *dynamic equilibrium* with which we are here concerned. This does not represent a state of rest, comparable with that of the boulder at the bottom of the hill or of the stable chemical compound, but a state of constant *activity* of the various parts of a *system*, activity which tends to maintain the characteristic configuration, internal structure, and autonomy of the system and also a more or less constant relationship with its environment. Very many such physical systems are known, but the conception may be applied also not only to biological but to psychological, social, economic and political entities.

Probably there are no physical systems in *perfect* equilibrium, i.e. they do not maintain themselves *indefinitely*, since some of their activities tend increasingly to disturb the adjustment of the whole. Biological and, even more, social and political systems are notably unstable because they always contain discordant elements whose activity makes, not for increasing equilibrium, but for disruption. Some aggregations of elements which show indications of system-formation are so imperfect in organization that we can hardly consider them as systems at all. But everywhere there is a *tendency* to the formation of systems with the establishment of dynamic equilibrium, flowing from the universal laws of the distribution of energy; and some systems show considerable autonomy and stability, resisting disturbance and maintaining at least an approach to dynamic equilibrium for a long time, while others are continually being destroyed and reconstructed in the same or in some modified form.

The universe may be thought of as containing innumerable

systems of every kind, shape and size in various stages of
development, each tending towards a dynamic equilibrium,
and others in various stages of disintegration when their equilibrium has broken down. Physical systems range from great
astronomical entities, of which our 'solar system' is a very
small example, down to the chemical atom, perhaps the most
stable of all physical systems, though it also is open to disintegration, either spontaneously, as in the case of the large
atoms of radium, or by the impact of external electronic
particles. Larger physical systems include great numbers of
smaller ones, while many systems overlap and intersect in
space in the most various ways, without losing their essential
autonomy. Many of them are highly unstable: systems are
constantly being destroyed either from inherent instability or
by the operation of external forces. The universe is littered
with the wrecks of systems which have disintegrated or been
destroyed, and the minute portion of it represented by the
surface of our planet is littered with others on a smaller scale.
But everywhere we find the appearance of fresh organization,
the initiation of new systems from the remains of old ones,
the re-establishment of old types of organization or the establishment of fresh ones in response to the universal tendency to
establish equilibrium in the play of forces, either a lifeless
and static, or an organized dynamic equilibrium.

   An individual living organism is a type of system that is
very characteristic and indeed unique. The higher organisms
are extremely complex and highly integrated and each main-
tains what seems to be a wonderfully perfect dynamic equilibrium for a certain period, but each contains within itself
the seeds of its own decay. Eventually its living equilibrium
ceases to be maintained—in other words it dies—its organization disintegrates, and its constituents pass into other relationships. The development of an individual organism from
the unicellular egg or spore to the mature state is the progress
of this unique system towards a temporary dynamic equi-

librium. At first the internal processes are not in equilibrium, and the continuous supply of raw material to the system in the form of food with its contained potential energy results in continuous assimilation and growth, increase in size and complexity of organization, until a position of equilibrium determined by the definite innate character of the species, carried by the genes, is attained. This mature condition is maintained for a longer or shorter time—the specific length of life—till internal changes begin which lead to senility and eventually to 'natural' death—the breakdown of the dynamic equilibrium. Some limit to the length of life of the individuals of a species is perhaps itself determined by natural selection— the lives of individuals if indefinitely prolonged would obviously militate against the continued success of the species.

The appearance of a *new* species by the acquirement of new characters in part of a population is brought about in various ways, but the new characters, or the modifications of old ones, have to be sufficiently adjusted to the existing environment to ensure the survival of the organism. The new characters may be indifferent to the life of the organism and in that case equilibrium with the environment is not disturbed; but new species are usually produced as the result of change in the conditions of life, the appearance of a new factor in the environment, or the spread of the species to a new habitat, and the new characters which arise are consequently subjected to a fresh selection, so that a new adjustment is established. Thus the appearance of a new species usually means the establishment of a new equilibrium between the systems represented by the individuals of which it is composed and their changed environment. The change is teleological, the end being the new equilibrium.

A *species* of plant or animal, i.e. the aggregate of all the individuals showing what are called the 'specific characters' which mark it off from other closely allied species, is not of course a 'system', though each individual is. But the aggre-

gations of different species of plants living side by side in the
same habitat, together with accompanying animals and all the
inorganic factors, such as the elements of climate and soil, to
which they are exposed, are true systems, though comparatively loosely integrated. Here we are concerned with the
establishment of those composite organic units which we call
plant associations or communities, such for instance as the
deciduous forest of central and western Europe, or the rain
forest of the wet tropics, or the grass vegetation of the south
Russian steppes or of the American prairies. Each of these
forms the basis of a characteristic assemblage of animals and
plants, continuously living together and maintaining, as a
whole, a dynamic equilibrium.

The deciduous forest of central and western Europe is
adapted as a whole to life in the central and western European
climate with which it is in equilibrium, and it can apparently
maintain itself indefinitely, under the prevailing conditions—
apart from human interference: only a marked change of
climate would replace it by another type. We know that this
is so from the history of the plant communities which have
followed one another in northern and central Europe, corresponding with climatic changes, since the end of the last Ice
Age. Such a great plant community as the European deciduous
forest includes within its limits many smaller communities,
and the same may be said of many other comparable plant
communities adjusted to the different climates of the world.
Each of these communities forms, together with the associated
animals and the given factors of climate, soil and water
supply, an equilibrated system which may be called an 'eco-
system'[1]. The development of new eco-systems can be traced
following marked changes of climate or any other radical
changes in the habitat.

With the necessary qualifications similar considerations

[1] From the Greek word οἶκος for a house or home, because it is a system
based on the natural home of the vegetation and the animals concerned.

apply to the well-integrated communities of mankind which have established a viable life of their own. These human communities are of course much more complex and far more highly integrated than those formed by most plants and animals (though bees, ants and termites form communities even more highly integrated than human societies) and they maintain substantial dynamic equilibrium, both internally and externally, for considerable periods and thus fall within the wide definition of a 'system'. The internal equilibrium of a human community may break down as the result of internal weaknesses, for example, extreme oppression of one class by another in a stratified society leading to revolution, or of violent religious, political or economic conflict, or of failure to produce enough of the necessary direct or indirect means of subsistence. But these are mainly diseases of highly developed but overripe communities verging on the senile. It is likely that highly complex, over-civilized communities can never maintain themselves indefinitely, and always develop senility and die of old age (internal breakdown) like an individual animal or plant. A human community may also, of course, like an individual organism, be overwhelmed and destroyed by the external attack of a more powerful neighbour, often following on internal weakness due to one of the causes mentioned.

The development of communities of organisms, whether the mixed communities of plants and animals that we find everywhere in terrestrial nature, and the human communities, basically consisting of the human species alone,[1] is a teleological phenomenon in the same sense as the development of new species adapted to new conditions of life, the 'end' being the organized, mature, self-maintaining com-

---

[1] Cultivated plants such as wheat or rice and domestic animals such as sheep and cattle may be essential parts of the human economy and therefore of the system. In the same way aphids or certain fungi may be essential to the economy of certain species of ants and are 'kept' by the communities of ants as 'domestic animals' or for food.

munity, just as the 'end' of the appearance of new forms in a population may be the successful segregation and establishment of a new species.

We can thus subsume all teleological development in nature under the general concept of the tendency towards the establishment of equilibrium which is a universal physical law. Not only so, but the conscious pursuit of an end by a human being falls within the same concept, though here the play of forces is mental. When a man makes up his mind to pursue a definite end, great or small, he is striving to fill an unsatisfied need which indicates an unstable distribution of psychic energy, in other words to attain a position of equilibrium in regard to the psychic elements concerned. If he is successful in attaining the end in view he gains a definite satisfaction, which represents a position of equilibrium or relative repose in regard to those elements, albeit often temporary. We can trace these activities of the human mind back into the satisfactions of instinct which (as we have seen in earlier chapters) are the bases of human psychical organization, and which were originally, and are largely still, unconsciously motivated. The human mind, as well as nature at large, is so complex and so full of free energy unfixed in definite, relatively stable systems, that it often gives the impression of a meaningless chaos, but the universal *tendency* within this seeming chaos to the establishment of equilibria, to organization in systems, is unmistakable, and is always revealed under close investigation.

There are many thinkers who see everywhere, not only in the mind of man, but in nature at large, evidence of *purpose*, so that they stress the teleological principle as fundamental. It does not seem strictly legitimate however to use the idea of purpose outside conscious human (or divine) thought, and even such purposive thought may be brought, as we have seen, within the general law of tendency towards the attainment of equilibrium. All causation exemplifies the universal law of trend towards equilibrium, but teleological causation exemplifies it in a special way, often shown in the tendency to the establishment of those dynamic equilibria which we call 'systems'. On the view that the universe is marching inevitably towards the equal distribution of energy postulated by the second law of thermodynamics these systems, in so far as they attain some sort of dynamic equilibrium, would represent temporary interruptions in the progress of entropy towards universal static uniformity.

CHAPTER 8

LOVE AND SEX

INNUMERABLE PEOPLE, through the centuries—minstrels
and poets, philosophers, theologians and psychologists, cynics
and philanthropists—have sung and written and spoken about
love, and there is no great human activity about which more
incompatible and contradictory things have been said—and,
incidentally, about which so much nonsense has been written.

Primarily this is because the *essence* of love has meant different things to different people. There are those to whom
love means, first of all, sexual love, the attraction of man to
woman and of woman to man. 'To make love' has a well defined and well understood meaning; it is to 'court' a member
of the opposite sex, whether by words, looks and demeanour,
or by physical contacts, or by all at the same time. No one,
not the most abstract philosopher, the strictest divine, the
most idealistic philanthropist, would misunderstand the
phrase or deny its validity. But the philosopher, the philanthropist and the theologian *would* be likely to deny that the
kind of love which is 'made' in this way is the essence and
type of love considered as a universal principle. He would
probably say that sexual love is only one kind of love, adapted
to the biological needs of man, that love is a principle of the
universe, or of the human mind, or of the mind of God,
expressed and fulfilled in various ways, of which the sexual
love of man and woman is by no means the 'highest'. He
might contend that different kinds of love were of basically
different nature, for instance Eros, the love that is human,
contrasted with Agape, the divine love which men may share,
and whose consummation is mystic union with God.

What is the common factor or essence of love which has
caused the same word to be used for such very different

things? Light can be thrown on this question if we trace the origin and essence of human love to its biological foundations, seeking it far back in the history of life itself.

Primitive organisms (though probably not the most primitive of all), representatives of which still exist today, have the form of minute units of living substance (protoplasm) equipped with the means of independent life in water or other liquid, able to nourish themselves and usually to move about. These are the 'unicellular organisms', of many and very various kinds, so called because each consists of a tiny mass of living substance possessing a 'nucleus' or centre of organization containing the hereditary 'genes' in its midst. The unicellular organism is thus constituted like each of the units of living substance, or 'cells', of which the 'multicellular' bodies of the higher animals and plants are composed.

These primitive organisms propagate themselves by division of the whole body—the single cell—preceded by division of the cell-nucleus, so that two or more individuals are produced from a single parent. The offspring then acquire the characters and grow to the size typical of the species or kind of unicellular organism to which they belong.

This process of multiplication of individuals by simple division of the body is the original primitive mode of *reproduction* of unicellular organisms which secures the continuity of the species. It is interrupted at intervals by another process —*conjugation*—in which two individuals come into contact and usually fuse with one another completely to form a new cell, the *zygote*; or, in one group of unicellular animals, the two cells come into close contact, exchanging portions of their nuclear equipment and then separate again and continue to divide independently.[1] In the typical case ('syngamy'), however, the nuclei of the two fusing individuals combine to

[1] The complete fusion of two individuals to form a zygote is now usually called 'syngamy' by zoologists, the term 'conjugation' being restricted to the comparatively rare case of temporary union with exchange of nuclear material.

form the nucleus of the zygote, which thus carries hereditary contributions from each of the conjugating parents, and becomes, so to speak, the ancestor of the nuclei of all the subsequent generations of individuals formed by renewed divisions of the zygote and its descendants.

These two contrasted processes—reproduction by division, and syngamy (or conjugation)—often alternate in a kind of rhythm, each fusion being followed by a number of successive divisions. In the higher animals we have become so used to the intimate connection of the two processes and the absolute dependence of reproduction upon previous union that the plain man naturally fails to recognize the two processes as basically distinct, and indeed the actual opposites of one another. This distinction nevertheless carries with it, as we shall eventually see, important psychological implications.

There is good evidence that the multicellular bodies of the higher animals and plants were derived in evolution from unicellular forms as the result of the products of cell division remaining together and forming the differentiated 'tissues' (aggregations of cells) of the bodies of the higher organisms, instead of separating to form new single-celled individuals. The power of continued cell division is largely lost by the body cells of the higher animals, once the tissues are fully formed, though it is partially retained by some tissues and shows itself by fresh cell divisions at a later period, often used as a means of at least partial regeneration of parts of the body lost by wounding or by disease.

But certain cells within the body retain the full power of division and of reproducing the species. These are the so-called *germ cells* which in due course fuse in pairs like the unicellular organisms which were their remote ancestors, producing *zygotes* from which the new individuals of the species develop. The germ cells are liberated from the body either before or after syngamy, though in the highest forms, both of animals and plants, one of the two fusing germ cells is always retained in the body of the parent so that the other has to be brought to it before fusion can occur. Thus the zygote develops into the embryo of the new organism within the body of one of the parents.

To return to the syngamy of unicellular organisms. In some forms the cells which fuse are, as described, the ordinary individuals of the species, but in many others the ordinary (vegetative) cells do not themselves conjugate but divide up into a number of others resembling the ordinary individuals but smaller and often simpler in structure. These last are then the actual conjugating cells and are called *gametes*. In some forms the gametes are of equal size and all alike, but very often they are of two kinds, one small, very active and highly sensitive (*male*), and the other relatively large and passive (*female*). The small active gametes are chemically attracted by the large ones, so that a pair of gametes—one small and one large—come into contact and fuse to form a zygote just as do gametes which are of equal size. This difference in size and activity of the gametes is the first appearance of *sex*, the differentiation of male and female gametes, in the evolutionary series.

The differentiation of sex persists in all the higher animals and plants, the germ cells (gametes) of which are always male and female. In some unicellular forms the male and female gametes have a general resemblance, both to one another and to the 'vegetative' (i.e. the non-conjugating) cells or individuals of the species to which they belong. But in many unicellular forms and in all the higher organisms the differentiation is extreme, the female gamete (*ovum* or 'egg') being relatively passive,[1] usually spherical, and in some forms containing stored food for the benefit of the new organism that will develop from the zygote; while the male gamete (*sperm*) is usually very slender and much elongated, extremely

---

[1] In some forms the ovum is active in the process of fusion, sending out a cone of protoplasm which catches and engulfs the male gamete.

active and sensitive to chemical stimuli, but so reduced and specialized in structure compared with the ordinary 'vegetative' cell that it is unable to feed itself or to survive for long after it has been liberated, unless it is kept at a suitable temperature in a special nutritive medium. The function of the male gamete or sperm is simply to carry bearers of the heredity of the species (*genes*) contained in its nucleus to the ovum or female gamete, where they remain side by side with corresponding genes contained in the nucleus of the ovum (egg). In this way the male and female make equal hereditary contributions to the offspring. The body of the sperm is either completely absorbed in the body of the egg when fusion occurs and the nuclei unite, or the non-nuclear portion of the sperm is cast off and disintegrates. The act of nuclear combination is usually known, in the higher organisms, as the *fertilization* of the egg by the sperm. But it is, as we have seen, in reality simply the union of two highly differentiated gametes, both ultimately derived from, and representing, two unicellular individuals of a very remote ancestor.

In the higher plants and animals elaborate bodily structures have been developed to ensure the successful transmission of sperms to eggs, and in the great majority of animals (including all the higher forms) the gametes of the two sexes are carried by separate individuals of the species, *the male and female individuals*, the structure and behaviour of whose bodies are adapted to the sexual function. In the highest animals, as we have seen, the female gametes are retained within the body of the female individual, and in the mammals, for example, in order to ensure safe transmission of the delicate short-lived sperms to the eggs the male individual must come into the most intimate contact with the female, involving 'coitus', a temporary 'union', as it is often called, of the bodies of the mates.

What do we learn from this whole series of biological facts? First that a great variety of unicellular organisms, from which we must believe that all the higher forms of life have been derived in evolution, are impelled to seek through chemical attraction or otherwise, first contact, and then complete union (fusion), with other individuals of their kind, and that from the results of these fusions succeeding generations of the species are produced. Secondly, that when multicellular organisms came into existence, some of their cells (germ cells) retained this power of union with others and the consequent production of offspring. Thirdly, that in many unicellular, and in all the higher multicellular forms of life the actual cells (gametes) which unite in this way are differentiated into small active (male) cells (sperms) and larger passive (female) cells (eggs), and that this differentiation is the basis of what we mean by sex. Fourthly, that in the higher animals sexual differentiation extends from the gametes to the bodies of the individuals which carry them, and not only to their bodies but to their minds, so that just as the male gametes of lower forms of life are impelled to seek and fuse with the female gametes, so the male individuals of the higher forms are impelled to seek out and enter into temporary union with the female individuals for the biological 'purpose' of transmitting the sperms which he carries and enabling one of them to come into contact with an egg produced by the female.

What is the common feature in all these processes—processes which presumably began at a very early stage in the evolution of life upon the earth and which are fundamental to the continuation of life as we know it? It is the impulsion to *contact* and then to *union*, first between two cells and then between two bodies, sometimes rising, in the human being, to a yearning for contact, and even mystical union, between two minds. In the psychical sphere this is the essence of *love*. Its biologically necessary primary expression in man is sexual love, but it *may* extend far beyond this, through homosexual or asexual love and friendship for individuals, through love and loyalty to the family, to members of the community at large, to the whole human race, to the non-human world, and ultimately to the love of God and a seeking for mystical union with God.

That is why love has been conceived by philosophers and theologians as the great sustaining and unifying principle of the universe and as the very essence of the Being of God Himself. It is the great unifying principle of life and of mind, because it seeks, everywhere and always, contact and ultimately union,[1] and nowhere is this essence of love more clearly seen than in the biological prototype of love, the union of unicellular individuals or of gametes in the process of syngamy. For man, in his own experience, this primal biological love necessarily means the sexual relation, because his body and part of his mind are sexually organized; but, as we have seen in tracing the process of syngamy from its origin among unicellular forms of life, *sex* is a secondary thing—the original process consists of the contact and union of equal individuals or gametes. Contact and union are the aim of the love impulse, and that is why love can altogether transcend the sexual impulse as such and come to mean the striving for contact and union, not of body with body but of mind with mind.

'Union' of course means very different things according to the objects involved. Clearly one cannot love a landscape or a picture or a piece of music or a book in the way that one can love a woman. The modes and contents of the love impulse are infinitely various and may be very complex. But if the love is genuine and intense there is always the *feeling* of the desire for union, for oneness, with the beloved object. Nor can one love God in the same sense that one loves any material person or thing, but the longing for union with God, realized in spirit by the religious mystic, is unmistakable.

The confusion of love with sex has led to much misunderstanding and not a little needless controversy. On one side are

[1] Compare the view of Eryximachus in Plato's *Symposium*, see p. 27.

those who not only regard the sexual relation as by far the most important type of love activity, but look upon all other kinds of love as directly derived from sex or as more or less pale reflections of sex. At the other extreme are those who look upon the sex relation as a degraded form of love, with undesirable concomitants and implications. Such people may even shrink from the sex relation altogether as essentially 'dirty' and disgusting, though an unfortunate necessity if the race is to survive. One might suppose they would prefer to see all babies produced by artificial insemination, which would eliminate a large part of the 'dirty' associations of the normal sexual relation and reduce it to a quasi-surgical process. Both of these classes of extremists ignore the teachings of biology, the former because they see the essence of love as specifically derived from the sexual relation instead of as the primal urge of living individuals to contact and union, the latter because they fail to realize that the sexual relation in man is of overwhelming importance to his psychical well-being, since it is the biologically conditioned channel through which all but the most exceptional people can express their human love with the greatest completeness and satisfaction. The second class, too, may fairly be charged with a definitely pathological bias, the origin and nature of which may be clearly revealed by psychological analysis.

Let us consider a little more closely the relation of sex and love as it is seen in man. In its lowest form the sexual impulse is almost entirely physiological. It is set in motion by the secretion of certain hormones[1] which have definite physiological effects leading to physical readiness for sexual intercourse. The physiological process is certainly accompanied by psychical elements, but these do not touch the higher mental functions of the personality. The man or woman in

[1] Definite chemical substances secreted by certain glands (secretory organs), released into the blood stream, and producing different specific physiological effects.

this condition is *prima facie* ready for intercourse with any member of the opposite sex, or even for a substituted action. Of course many and various inhibiting factors are most often brought into play and prevent the carrying out of the function.

A higher level is reached when there is a specific desire for a particular person of the opposite sex. The urge is then focused on a particular sexual object, and cannot, for the moment at least, be diverted from it. A man is said, in the old direct phrase, to 'lust after' a particular woman, and for the time being nothing and no one else will do. Lust is not love, as has been truly said over and over again, and not only by moralists. Nevertheless it is the biological and psychological foundation of sexual love between individual men and women, an extension of the primeval urge to unite of unicellular individuals or gametes to highly developed, sexually differentiated human organisms.

Psychical factors now come prominently into the picture, far more prominently than at the lower level where the sexual urge is unfocused. Attraction of a man to a particular woman or of a woman to a particular man necessarily arises through the senses and may possess the mind to the exclusion of everything else. It may lead to psychical processes remote from the primitive sexual urge, for example to idealization of the sexual object, or to ardent desire for a union of minds, or to an overwhelming urge to secure the well-being and happiness of the beloved object at any cost to the self—a characteristic which has often been cited as the essential feature of personal love in the higher sense.

It is a striking fact that this unselfish altruistic love is often characteristic of the 'first love' of an adolescent boy or girl, (at least in western civilization), in which physical desire is thrust into the background. If present, as it probably always is, the longing for physical union may remain at first completely unconscious while the mental and spiritual elements of the attraction are prominent. It is easy to attribute this state of mind to early education in which the physical aspect of sexual love is taboo, so that it is repressed by the super-ego. In this way a strong, even passionate, sentiment may be built up while its instinctive basis is ignored. But there has been little attempt at detailed psychological analysis of this phase of love between the sexes.

It is in altruism that love in the higher sense emerges from primitive sexual attraction. We saw at the outset that 'to make love' has a universally recognized and well understood meaning as the actions involved in the efforts towards physical union of two human beings. On a higher plane and in a wider sense this union comes to mean something far transcending the physical, and far wider than the sex relation, though we cannot ignore its origin and prototype. The impulse of love may extend to any human being, to the whole human race, to objects of the non-human world, to non-material things such as 'causes' or 'ideals', and ultimately to God Himself. In all these, as we saw, the essence of it is the urge to *union*, which may finally be expressed in the desire to be merged in a great entity or whole, such as we see especially in some eastern religions.

The biological fact that reproduction and syngamy are in origin and essence two distinct and indeed opposed processes (since one involves separation, the union union) though in the higher animals the former, which is historically prior, has come to depend absolutely on the latter, is reflected in different psychological attitudes towards mating and towards producing children. Many human beings ardently desire sexual union without wishing to procreate children, though that is the normal consequence of the fulfilment of their desire. Many women, through 'maternal' instinct, greatly desire children but have little interest in sexual intercourse. The social problems arising from this distinctness and from the modern attempts to separate the two processes by the extensive use of contraceptives are well known and it is no part of

our purpose to discuss the advantages and drawbacks of con-
traception. But the psychological distinctness corresponding
with the primitive biological distinctness of the two functions, closely connected though they are through the normal
biological sequence of union and division of cells, especially
in the higher animals, must be insisted upon. To represent
the physical pleasure of sexual intercourse as a 'bait' devised
by Nature to lure human beings into parentage and its obliga-
tions is to misconceive the psychological basis and the essential nature of the first function. The overwhelming desire for
union as such is an expression of a primitive urge, the
prototype of all love. And when transferred to the whole
human organism it has its own values, both biological and
spiritual, and exists, so to speak, in its own right.

The doctrine that all sexual intercourse should be directed
to procreation is especially characteristic of the Roman
Catholic Church. It is, of course, bound up with the desire to
safeguard the stability and fertility of marriage carrying the
religious sanction (which is given the status of a sacrament)
by a strict moral code which proclaims the procreation of
children as the primary object of marriage and condemns as
sin not only all extra-marital intercourse but all use of contraceptives within the marriage bond. It is, however, also
bound up with, and probably owes its primary motive to, the
dislike and fear of the sexual relationship itself which tinges
nearly the whole of orthodox Christianity. This is notably
developed in Puritanism as the fear and hatred of the 'carnal
lusts' and finds its extreme form in that horrified shrinking
from the sexual relation as essentially dirty and disgusting
already alluded to. 'Since unfortunately we must have sexual
intercourse if the race is to continue', the Puritan might be
thought of as saying, 'let us restrict it under penalty to
narrow channels which have been duly sanctioned by
authority.'

The mental association of sex with dirt is deeply embedded

in modern western culture, as common language sufficiently testifies—'a dirty story', 'a clean-living man', and so on.[1] Without considering the detailed explanations of this association offered by psycho-analytic theory we may safely attribute it partly to the use of a single channel for both genital and excretory products as well as to the nearness of the defecatory end of the intestine to the external urino-genital organs. The close anatomical and physiological relations of the genital and excretory organs and functions have thus led to the 'smearing', as it were, of the sexual function with excretory and defecatory 'dirt'. No doubt there are other psychological factors involved, but to discuss them here would lead us too far afield.

Separate and distinct as are the nature and values of reproduction and sexual union, there can be no doubt that a love marriage, passing into a deep mutual understanding and a securely rooted mutual affection 'when passion's trance is overpast', if it can be achieved, is the most permanently satisfactory and the completest form of the sexual relationship, just because it is a permanent lifelong union. And an essential part of it, of course, is the normal biological sequence of intercourse and the conception and bearing of children. But the primary sex attraction and its issue in coitus has an immediate and independent value of the highest importance, both physiological and psychological, dependent on its culmination in mutual orgasm. It is the fullest biological satisfaction of the need for contact and union, the primary love

[1] It may be argued that a 'clean-living' man is not required to abstain from sexual intercourse with his wife, and that the implication of the phrase does not refer to the physical function of sex but to the 'moral dirt' involved in illicit intercourse, which is 'sin'. That this is a secondary intention of the phrase may be admitted, but other and more grievous sins are not regarded as specially 'dirty', though it is true that 'sharp practice' or double dealing for one's own advantage is often called a 'dirty trick', and here the metaphor is certainly purely ethical. The epithet 'dirty' applied to sexual sins attaches to the sexual process itself, the physical process, and the emotion behind it is seen in its extreme form in the puritans who do feel that all sexual processes are 'dirty'.

instinct: and potentially the love instinct, in its general sense, is, on all counts, at once the widest, the deepest, and the highest of human experiences.

A stable marriage is the only really satisfactory background for the rearing of children healthy in body and mind. The basic importance of the family as the prototype of human community relationships is described in Chapter 10. That the family is the essential unit of a stable society is profoundly true, and there can be no more important social and political function than the provision of conditions which favour the establishment and maintenance of secure families. Of recent years there has been a great deal of penetrating study of the psychological relationships between the different members of a family, and there is now available an ample and enlightening literature on the subject. In the early life of the child are laid the foundations of his potentialities of future happiness and success, and when his family relationships go awry the seeds of future misery and tragedy are sown.

CHAPTER 9

THE STRENGTH AND WEAKNESS OF PSYCHO-ANALYSIS

NO ONE can deny that the development and spread of psycho-analysis has had a profound influence on the thought of the world during the last fifty years and especially since the first world war. Working in Vienna practically alone during the nineties of the last century, Freud was laying its foundations, and in the first two decades of this he was actively developing its structure and gathering disciples and fellow-workers around him. During this time also there were two important schisms in the group of psychologists and psychiatrists whom Freud had attracted to the new doctrines. In Vienna itself Adler, and in Zurich Jung, disagreed with certain fundamental tenets of Freud's system, and each founded a school of his own, later called 'Individual' and 'Analytical' Psychology respectively. Since then various others who were originally Freud's disciples have broken away from his school on different points, but few of their contributions have any great importance. Into the details of these divergences it is not proposed to enter here: both Adler and Jung propounded ideas of considerable value and each found many disciples in different countries, so that a good deal of psychiatric work is now carried on according to their respective tenets. But it is Freud's original school which represents the central line of development of the subject, which commands by far the greatest number of adherents all over the world, and to which the name psycho-analysis is properly restricted by fairly general consent. The term 'psychological analysis' ('deep' analysis) may be used in the more general sense. After the first world war, and to an important degree as an effect of its experiences, the results of Freudian analysis became very widely known and began to exercise a profound influence not only on psychiatry and psychology but in many other fields of thought.

A change in the general estimate of the relative powers in human motivation of instinct and emotion on the one hand, and of the rational faculty on the other, was the most important aspect of this influence. Not that there was anything new in the view that men are not governed primarily by reason—many thinkers had been insisting through the centuries that prejudice and passion were the real determinants of most men's opinions and the most potent driving forces of their actions. What Freud's work did was to uncover and analyse some of the psychical forces at work and to demonstrate the ways in which they acted. Starting from the cases of psycho-neurotics—in the first instance of hysterics—he traced the causes of their symptoms to specific emotional disturbances which had been completely repressed and forgotten and could only be recalled under hypnosis or by persistent recourse to the method of 'free association'. In this last characteristic psycho-analytic technique the patient speaks of whatever comes to the surface of consciousness, and since the psychical trouble he is suffering from is his most insistent concern, all or most of his conscious thoughts during the analytic interview relate in some way to this—though often very far from obviously. By devious paths and often only after a long time the root of the trouble, i.e. an emotional conflict or disturbance, is revealed (in successful analysis) as the cause of the symptoms, and the way in which it has acted is made clear. In course of time Freud found that the emotional disturbances of adult life, which were the proximate causes of the neurotic symptoms, themselves had antecedents in earlier events of related character and that the chains of causation invariably extended back to early childhood. On the basis of long continued and laborious clinical work he concluded that neurotic symptoms were ultimately due to the persistent effects of the primitive reactions of the infant and the young child to its environment, and of the fantasies to which these reactions gave rise, particularly reactions to the significant figures in that environment, in the first place to the mother, then to the father, and possibly to other members of the family. These infantile experiences had been incorporated in the structure of the mind and had thus determined the mental reactions of the individual to adult situations.

It soon became clear that these motivations and mechanisms were by no means confined to neurotics, but that they were shared by 'normal' minds and personalities, and could be traced in every kind of human thought and activity—in myths and legends, in religion, philosophy and creative art, as well as in the habits and the eccentricities of everyday life. Of the actual origin and nature of such motivations the individual is normally quite unconscious, and to explain this fact Freud postulated an unconscious level of the mind into which the memories of the significant early experiences had been 'repressed' because of their unpleasant or their horrifying nature, as described in Chapter 2.

Again, the conception of an unconscious part of the mind was not new. What Freud did was to make it more definite and to show that it was a necessary postulate to explain his clinical results. Thus he replaced vague conceptions by what may fairly be called scientific demonstrations of actual psychical mechanisms. His essential contribution may be compared with Darwin's to the theory of evolution. The theory itself was not new, but Darwin was the first to demonstrate an actual mechanism by which it could be brought about. In both cases this was the decisive factor leading to widespread conviction of the truth of the conception. In both cases the effect on human thought was revolutionary and met with obstinate opposition, because the new doctrines upset traditional and cherished beliefs.

The great significance of early childhood as the period in

which the foundations of psychoneurosis are laid down is the result of the utter dependence of the body and mind of the infant on those who tend it, primarily the mother. The relations of the infant and young child to its mother are in the first place physical relations of the highest possible degree of intimacy. The child has been born into the world through its mother's vagina after nine months of development within her uterus, and it depends during the first months of its extra-uterine life upon its mother's milk and upon the warmth of her body for essential food, comfort and satisfaction, i.e. for its primary physical and psychical needs. These basic physical relations involve the mother's primary and secondary sexual organs, and the psychical relations arising immediately from them are quite clearly of the same sort of stuff as the psycho-sexual relation between man and woman. For these reasons Freud thought of the attitude of the child to its mother as a sexual attitude, and brought the whole of the child's relations to father and mother within the sphere of sex, centering round the famous 'Oedipus complex'. The psychic energy involved was called 'libido', identified with the human urge to love and desire, and made the foundation not only of all human affection but of the vital creative activities of adult life, however remote these might be from sexual activity in the ordinary sense.

It has always seemed to the author that this was an unfortunate use of language. It is true enough that all these psychical manifestations have something in common and particularly that the child's primary psychical relation to its mother is, as has been said, 'of the same sort of stuff' as the psycho-sexual relation: furthermore that the Oedipus situation, when it is well developed, does seem to involve direct sexual desire (albeit in an infantile form) as well as hostility to a rival. It is currently admitted that the specific sexual urge does not, as used to be thought, appear suddenly at the age of puberty, but that it can be plainly seen, though of course in a rudimentary form, in very young children. 'Infantile sexuality', so vehemently repudiated when Freud first wrote on the subject, is evident enough now to all who are closely concerned with bringing up young children. Nevertheless the denotation of the word sex and its equivalents should not be widened from its ordinary meaning (which applies in all languages only to the differentiation between male and female and the specific relation which it determines) to include all the affective relations between parents and offspring. The word *love* is properly applied to a far wider conception, as was argued in detail in Chapter 8: its essence is the urge to *union*. The specific sex relation is the most important biological channel through which this urge finds expression, but it cannot properly be *identified* with the urge to union at large, nor can the primary relation of the infant to its mother be included in the narrower concept. The infant-mother relation is of the same stuff as sex, but it is not the same thing as sex, though it may, as in the Oedipus situation, run into the specifically sexual channel.

This misapplication of a word which Freud adopted has unfortunately been maintained by orthodox psycho-analysts, and has been the cause of many critical attacks, though these have seldom been directed to the cause and essence of the mistake. It has been argued by psycho-analysts on the other hand that if Freud chose to employ the word sex with a wider denotation than that of ordinary language the deviation was not important, provided the meaning he attached to it was clearly understood. It has even been argued by one eminent psycho-analyst that what Freud did was to *discover* sex in all these relations just as the chemists discovered nitrogen not only as a free gas in the atmosphere, but also as forming part of the structure of the molecules of nitric acid, for example, and of proteins. Freud did in fact discover a common governing element in all these psychical processes, but that common element was not sex in its ordinary and well-understood meaning: it was the urge to union in living beings, which has unfortunately no appropriate technical name, but which expresses itself in what we know as love on the higher as well as on the lower psychical planes. As a universal principle Freud later on called it *Eros* from the name of the Greek god of love and that would be appropriate enough, since Plato used it quite generally for all kinds of love. But unfortunately the adjective *erotic* is now firmly associated in ordinary language with sex in the narrow sense, and it has become impossible to apply it, as Alexander has recently proposed, to all *spontaneous* discharges of psychic energy (see p. 27).

The charge of 'pansexualism' which has often been brought against Freudian psychology is thus seen to have a certain justification, and pansexualism has done the psycho-analytic movement a good deal of harm, because of the 'sex taboo' arising from the fear of sex and the widespread repression of sexual ideas on which psycho-analysis has thrown so much light. The hostility aroused in this way would have been largely avoided if the more general conception of love as the urge to union, instead of a word conveying a sharply defined and much narrower concept, had been made the basis of exposition. It must, however, still be remembered that sex in the strict sense *is* the most important *biological* channel of human love and does figure largely in very early life, both in general infantile sexuality and particularly in the Oedipus complex.

The phenomena of homosexuality are very relevant to this question. There can be no doubt that physical homosexual relations between two people of the same sex are a direct substitute for the normal physical heterosexual relation and are quite properly considered as sexual 'perversion'. There are, however, all degrees of homosexuality, varying from the extreme form in people who may be called compulsive homosexuals, and who are quite incapable of heterosexual activity

—a condition often associated with paranoiac[1] tendencies—to people who merely feel a slight physical attraction to certain members of their own sex, an attraction which is faint and transient but can still be clearly recognized as of the same nature as the normal heterosexual impulse. Excluding the fixed compulsive type, many homosexuals are equally capable of heterosexual activity and may in fact engage in physical relations with either sex when they can find willing partners. This 'ambisexual' disposition can be envisaged simply as an overflow of sexual energy beyond the normal biological channels.

But here we must take into account the 'bisexual' nature of the human organism. There is abundant evidence of the existence of masculine impulses in women and of feminine impulses in men, and this fact is now much easier to understand as the result of modern work on the nature and effects of the sex hormones in determining sexual activity as well as primary and secondary sexual characters. In the great majority of men, of course, the masculine tendencies predominate, in accord with bodily structure and functions, and in most women the feminine. But in a good many people some of the characteristic traits of the opposite sex are pronounced. Even in quite masculine men, occasional evidence of feminine traits may be traced, and similarly masculine traits in quite feminine women. Characteristics of the opposite sex may be strongly repressed and only become clearly apparent when unconscious impulses are able to come to the surface in symbolized forms, as in dreams. The social pressure on the young man to behave overtly in a 'manly', and on the young woman in a 'womanly' way, is very considerable, though not so overwhelming as it used to be.

But men who are thoroughly feminine both in appearance

---

[1] Paranoia is a form of insanity in which grandiose delusions about the personality, delusions of persecution and the habit of 'projecting' internal psychical phenomena upon others are conspicuous symptoms.

and disposition, and women who are markedly masculine, are well enough known, and it is usually, though not always, among these that the most pronounced cases of homosexuality are met with. In male homosexuality the passive partner is of the feminine type—usually young and often a mere boy—while the active partner may be aggressively masculine, and very often heterosexual as well as homosexual.[1] In female homosexuality the active partner often has pronounced masculine traits. Cases of two women who are intimate friends and live together, and one of whom is of decidedly masculine type, taking the lead in all joint activities, are common enough, and may or may not be accompanied by physical homosexuality. Even in 'normal' heterosexual intercourse certain women display something of the aggressiveness usually associated with the male partner.

These manifestations of the overflow of sex beyond the limits of the normal sex-relation conditioned by bodily structure might be thought to justify the attribution of all emotional affection to the sexual impulse. But specific homosexuality depends for its existence on the normal male-female antithesis: its actual physical manifestations can only be interpreted in terms of normal sex, of which it is a 'perversion', and this is not true of human affection at large. Though the urge to contact and union is first seen in evolution in the contact and union of cells, and afterwards of complex bodies, the universal emotion of love, is in principle free from all physical limitations. If it is not definitely sexual to begin with

[1] Something like this seems to have been the standard psycho-sexual bent among the Athenians of Socrates' circle, the difference between our attitude and theirs being that they exalted and idealized the homosexual relation with boys and depreciated the heterosexual (which they regarded as on a lower plane) while we tend to view the former with disgust and to romanticize the latter. The Athenian homosexual relation to boys was not necessarily or entirely physical, the mental aspect being often stressed. But the boy friend was certainly regarded by the older man as a specific love-object in the same sense as a person of the opposite sex is with us.

it may run into the biological and physical channels, either normal or abnormal—in other words it may easily *become* sexual—but to call it sexual *in essence* can only be regarded as a misuse of language. A man or woman *may* love another human being of either sex without any trace of specifically sexual impulse, and in that case the love is neither homosexual nor heterosexual but asexual, and often almost purely mental or spiritual.

Besides his widening of the concept of sex to include all kinds of affection Freud extended it in another way. He found among young children specific emotions connected with the taking of food—at first the sucking of the mother's milk—and with the defecatory and excretory functions, so that these emotions were associated specifically with the corresponding organs—mouth, rectum and anus, and urethra. The natural feelings and urges connected with these necessary functions Freud described as 'partial sexual' urges, contributing to the building up of the adult psycho-sexual complex and crowned at puberty by the full development of the specifically 'genital' urge which finds its goal in coitus. Each of these 'partial urges'—oral, anal and urethral—Freud found to be associated with certain psychical characteristics, and when one-sidedly developed to be connected with particular types of character. Fixation of the psyche on individual 'partial urges' might also lead to well known types of sexual perversion, or alternatively to neurosis as the result of repression.

These astonishing conclusions naturally excited a great deal of hostile criticism, often contemptuous and derisive, but nevertheless the clinical evidence for the substance of Freud's thesis cannot be ignored. The contribution of the psychical aspects of nutritive and excretory functions to the adult psycho-sexual complex becomes more intelligible when we consider the type of sensitivity common to the mucous membranes of lips, mouth and tongue, nipples, anus and rectum, in addition to the primary sexual organs—vulva, clitoris,

vagina, glans, urethra and scrotum—and to the skin sur-
rounding these organs,[1] all tending to react sexually to
various stimuli, so that they have been called 'erogenous
zones'. It is this physiological link which is the basis of the
close association of the psychical concomitants of primary
nutritive and excretory functions with those of the sexual function, and which gives the former their status as 'partial' or
contributory factors in the formation of the characteristic
sexual affect-complex when it has been completed by the full
development of the specific genital component. One aspect
of this close connection—the 'smearing' of the sexual function with the psychical repulsion to excretory products—
has already been discussed in Chapter 8, and another is the
employment of extra-sexual 'erogenous' organs in the sexual
perversions as well as in the caresses of lovers. Freud's syn-
thetic work on this topic is in fact one of his most brilliant
achievements and naturally reinforced in his mind his wide
extension of the concept of sex. Just as on the higher psychical
level sexual love is of the same basic stuff as other kinds of
love—a yearning for contact and union—so on this psycho-
somatic level the apertures of the body which subserve the
nutritive and defecatory functions share certain basic characteristics with the sexual apertures, while the external genital
organs are actually identical with the urinary. Again we want
a common term which could be applied to all and thus enable
us to avoid misuse of the word sexual.

Freud showed a general tendency to extend the denotation
of ordinary words (involving a decrease of their connotation)
till he arrived at a much more general idea than that conveyed
by their common use, and this habit has naturally led to misunderstanding, as the present writer pointed out many years
ago.[2] This is conspicuously seen in Freud's employment not

[1] The skin of the whole body tends to share this sensitivity, though in very
varying and usually much lesser degree.
[2] *The New Psychology and its Relation to Life*, Revised Edition, 1922, p. 12.

only of the word *sex*, but also of the words *wish* and *pleasure* (the 'pleasure principle'). He practically identifies 'wish' with what psychologists usually call 'conation', and 'pleasure' (German *Lust*) with 'release of mental tension'.

Now release of mental tension is certainly a universal principle of mental process. The mind constantly tries to release its tensions by the discharge of bound[1] psychic energy —the instinctive process (Chapter 5) is a typical example— thus reaching equilibrium and repose, just as physical energy behaves in a similar way, potential (bound) energy passing into kinetic (free) energy and thus dissipating itself. The specific sensation of pleasure or ease is a characteristic accompaniment of this process, as when we eat and drink to satisfy our hunger and thirst and get pleasure from the process, or, in the cognitive sphere, when we succeed in solving a troublesome problem which has created tension in the mind. But release of mental tension is a far more general conception, and if we *identify* it with the experience of pleasure we are compelled to accept the theory of psychological hedonism, which supposes that the pursuit of pleasure is the motive of all action. It has often been shown that pleasure, as such, is not, and cannot be, the *aim* or the *motive* of all action, but release of tension and the ease accompanying it are certainly characteristic and universal mental phenomena.[2]

It is perfectly true that remembered experience of pleasure and ease accompanying and following certain past actions are useful signs and may act as guides to fresh actions on the same lines. In this sense they are part of the causes of such actions. But the main causes, are the universal and continuing *impulse* to discharge bound energy, to release mental tension, in-

[1] I.e. psychic energy immediately at the disposal of an unsatisfied urge, not to be confused with what psychoanalysts call 'fixated libido' which is usually unconscious and impossible to release except by special methods.

[2] The sensation of ease rather than that of pleasure is really more characteristic of the release of mental tension. Pleasure may also accompany the excitement often involved in the tension itself.

herent in the psyche and specially characteristic of the working of all the great instincts.

The flood of hostile criticism, often violent and unfair,
encountered by psycho-analysis in its earlier days had the
effect of consolidating its adherents into a closely-knit union
for the defence as well as for the propagation and further
development of its tenets, so that psycho-analysts as a body
rather came to resemble a persecuted sect or church, with a
strict orthodoxy, a united front against hostile critics, and a
great bitterness towards schisms that developed within it.
This had unfortunate results, because the atmosphere of a
persecuted church is of course quite alien from the atmosphere of objective science, and psycho-analysis claimed (quite
justifiably in the author's view) to be a branch of objective
science. Too many psycho-analysts resented all criticism of
their tenets and tended to look upon the words of Freud
rather as an old-fashioned devout Christian looked upon the
words of the Bible. To some extent this attitude still persists
and is sometimes associated with an attitude of superiority
towards benighted outsiders which is not devoid of arrogance.
But it did not, of course, extend to the more vigorous and
judicial minds among analysts, and there has in fact been considerable recent fresh development of the body of psycho-
analytic theory, most of it on sound lines. In later years,
particularly, there has also been a welcome effort to bring
psycho-analytic theory into relation with the results of other
branches of psychology, while psycho-analytic therapy has
been much more widely welcomed by the medical profession at large. Indeed a prominent analyst recently called
attention to the risks psycho-analysis ran from becoming
too respectable!

But there is still a tendency to adhere closely to Freud's
views on particular points which cannot be justified. One of
these is the inheritance of characters acquired by individuals

as the result of experiences during their lifetime, in which Freud firmly believed. As a general theory, at least, this is contrary to the evidence and is rejected by the great majority of biologists, so that it cannot legitimately be considered as a primary evolutionary factor. All we know of the mechanism of heredity contradicts its general validity, though it is still possible that something like it may occur as a partial phenomenon in a limited sphere. When some psycho-analysts speak of the 'inheritance' of the Oedipus complex they seem to misconceive the nature of heredity. All that can be strictly 'inherited' is a nervous and corresponding psychical mechanism which, under appropriate conditions, will develop the complex. But there is another sense in which the Oedipus complex may be 'inherited'—though not physically. The environment of a home in which one (or both) of the parents is conspicuously affected by the love, jealousy and hostility characteristic of the complex is eminently adapted to produce the same condition in the children.

Another belief that seems to be held by the majority of contemporary psycho-analysts, though not by all, is that 'instincts' may ultimately be resolved (or rather combined) into two—the 'life' and 'death' instincts or 'urges' (*Lebenstrieb* and *Todestrieb*). This schematization was propounded by Freud in *Jenseits des Lustprinzips* ('Beyond the Pleasure principle') in 1920, and the two supposed motive forces were afterwards known as *Eros* and *Thanatos*. These two have been equated at various times with *Love* and *Hate*, *Tenderness* and *Aggression*, *Constructiveness* and *Destructiveness*. The generalization in the human mind of these various pairs of polar opposites is of course inescapable,[1] but to call them fundamental 'Triebe' or 'instincts' to which all human (and indeed all biological) activity can be referred seems to get us nowhere at all. Freud tried to base his theory on biology, but his treatment of the

[1] Going back to Empedocles' cosmic theory which held Love to be the combining and Strife the disruptive force pervading the universe.

fundamental life processes reveals a failure to grasp the significance of the relevant biological data or to put them into
proper perspective, and his arguments are faulty and
tendentious.

The biological facts do not support the generalization. The
failure of life and the consequent break-up of living organic
structure into inorganic constitutents depend essentially on
the failure of the conditions, external or internal, necessary
to maintain life, the life of the organism as a whole, or of individual living cells, and cannot, as Freud suggests, be sub-
sumed under the concept of an 'urge' or 'instinct' to 'return
to the inorganic' in the psychophysical organism. And to
throw together all the characteristic vital activities, whether
physiological or psychical, into a single 'Lebenstrieb',
amounts to no more than saying, tautologically, that living
organisms display the various activities which make us recognize them as alive. The proper function of the concepts of
'urge' and 'instinct'[1] is to designate psycho-physical activities
of a particular type which can be separately recognized.

The conception of a 'Todestrieb' which urges every individual to pursue his life course, with death and the consequent
return to the inorganic as the ultimate *aim*, is far-fetched and
indeed fantastic; but a 'Todestrieb' is a real enough phenomenon in the minds of some ageing people who feel their
powers failing and that it is 'time to go', and most notably
of course in the minds of suicides and of very many 'normal'
people to whom the impulse to suicide is familiar but who

---

[1] It is undesirable to use 'instinct' as synonymous with 'urge' or 'drive'
(Trieb). Freud often rightly insisted that an 'urge' was essentially internal in
origin, that its appearance in the individual was not due to external stimuli. And
it is better to use the word instinct in McDougall's sense described in Chapter 5,
including the whole instinct mechanism, of which reaction to stimulus is an
essential part. Thus the vague feeling of unrest displayed by an adolescent of
either sex is often due to the usually unconscious sexual *urge*, while the overwhelming attraction to an individual of the opposite sex, whose acknowledged
or unacknowledged aim is coitus, represents the fully developed sex *instinct*.

never come within measurable distance of carrying it out. The causes of the suicidal impulse are diverse. Perhaps most often suicide is seen as the only means of ultimate *escape* from the strains and stresses of a world that has become too distressing for further endurance. Sometimes the resolution to kill oneself is taken as an escape from a specific unendurable evil, such as a painful and incurable disease or the threat of an overwhelming social disgrace. Sometimes it is a form of *revenge*, the most effective way of returning an injury, real or imagined. In other cases it may be a self-inflicted *punishment*—the capital punishment—for guilt. Here Freud is probably right in calling it an act of aggression directed against the self, comparable with the acts of retaliatory aggression represented by private revenge, or by the legal punishment inflicted on guilty criminals. The feeling of guilt which gives rise to the suicidal impulse as self-punishment is however very often unconscious, and the psychiatrist has to take account of this fact, as well as of the various possible conscious motives, when he is confronted with the self-destructive impulse in his patients. But increasingly common as this impulse may be in the difficult modern world it is certainly far from being universal.

Great genius as he was, Freud was no philosopher—he would have been the first to repudiate the title—but his work was concerned with such fundamental characters of the human mind that he was sometimes tempted into philosophizing—he called it 'metapsychology'. Freud's genius was that of the empirical scientist, though its field was far removed from the ordinary subject matter of natural science.

Psycho-analysis has illuminated the dark places of the unconscious mind in a remarkable way, and the light which it has thrown on obscure mental processes has given us a much truer picture of the human psyche as a whole. There are still those who persist in regarding psycho-analysis merely as a particular empirical psycho-therapeutic technique, but this attitude shows a wilful blindness to the results of Freud's exploration of the unconscious. Those results could not have had such far-reaching effects on thought throughout the civilized world nor could they have been successfully applied in fields lying far outside psychotherapy unless they had had real scientific validity for the normal human mind. It is noteworthy too how widely their truth has been more or less intuitively recognized by many men of broad and deep literary and humanistic culture who have given little or no special study to the subject.

The weaknesses of psycho-analysis are partly inherent in the nature of the material with which it deals. The phenomena are obscure and elusive, their elements are difficult to isolate, and controlled experiment is impossible. The analyst cannot exhibit his methods and results directly to other observers, since he and the analysand must be alone together because success in the work depends on the establishment of an intimate personal relationship between them. Furthermore, the presence and interventions of the analyst continually modify the reactions of the analysand, i.e. they necessarily alter the material with which the analyst is dealing. All these conditions inevitably open the door to mistakes and misconceptions as well as to emotionally determined faulty technique, since the material is constantly concerned with the emotions, and those of the analyst cannot be excluded. All these difficulties and pitfalls are quite apart from the obviously wide opportunities for incompetence and for quackery, against which indeed the recognized psycho-analytic clinics now take the most stringent precautions through a system of severe training of those who seek to enter the profession.

The soundness of postulated psychical mechanisms can in any case only be tested by repeated applications to successive cases, and the psychical processes at work thus gradually sifted out and formulated. The best testimony to the soundness of the main body of psycho-analytical theory is that the same reactions to the same or similar situations, the same patterns of behaviour, constantly recur, not only in the neurotic but in so-called 'normal' people; and recognized practising psycho-analysts for the most part agree that the concepts formed to resume them fit the psychical facts over a wider and wider range of experience.

The working of the unconscious mind, according to Freudian theory, is entirely strange not only to conscious modes of logical thought but to conscious emotions, and the unconscious uses imagery based on an extraordinary range of primitive symbolism. This is frequently extremely bizarre, completely alien from the conscious mental processes to which we are accustomed. Anyone freshly approaching the subject is therefore likely to find many of the accounts and explanations given by psycho-analysts incredible and even ridiculous. Some of them are certainly insufficiently established, inherently improbable, and may well turn out to be illusory. The subject does provide abundant temptation to overbold and unsupported speculation by minds which have more lively imagination than sober scientific judgment. Still it must be remembered that many of Freud's early conclusions, now well established, seemed at first very wild and fantastic. It is not open to the outsider to be sceptical of psychical phenomena of which he has no experience, as reported by psycho-analysts, or to condemn psycho-analytic theory because of its strangeness, any more than it is open to him to disbelieve the results of histology or cytology when he has never used a microscope.

Mistakes have been made and corrected, formulations have been modified or altered and new ones introduced, estimations of the relative importance of different phenomena have varied; and such changes will continue. Comparable modifications are characteristic of every developing branch of science: finality is never attained. With new discoveries and enlarged perspectives it may well be that the time will come when the phenomena of what we now call the unconscious mind will be expressed in different language, just as the language now used in describing ultimate physical phenomena is different from Newton's. But it is impossible to doubt that Freud's discoveries will remain part of the foundations of psychology, as the discoveries of Galileo and Newton have remained part of the foundations of astronomy and physics.

CHAPTER 10

THE FAMILY AND THE COMMUNITY

IT IS a commonplace that the family is the essential unit of
human society, at least of the traditional society that has come
down to us through the ages, though some of its functions are
now seriously threatened by increasing socialistic organization which is assuming more and more of the original respon-
sibilities of the family. But as so often happens with things
which are very familiar we may easily take the family too
much for granted and fail to realize the full significance and
the full implications of the thesis that the family is the essential unit of human society as we know it, and almost certainly
of any possible free and healthy community.

The ties that hold together the members of a family are
deeply rooted in biology and psychology and in the aggregate
are by far the most enduring of normal human ties. First of all
there is the sexual tie between husband and wife, an outcome
of one of the two strongest instincts of man. Following on this
comes the companionship and mutual support which the
partners can give one another when marriage is a life long
bond—potentially at least the firmest and most valuable of
human partnerships. Then there is the unique relation of the
mother to her children, involving at the outset the most intimate of all physical bonds between human beings and a psychical bond of special character which commonly lasts
throughout life. Second only to this is the relation of the
father to his children, not so intimate as the mother's, but
remarkably powerful. Finally there is the strong and valuable
emotional relationship of brothers and sisters.

Born and brought up under these continuing influences the
relation of children to parents is decisive for the formation of
their characters—subject of course to particular heredity—

and thus of their whole future lives. Though it is indeed plain enough, we often scarcely realize the full implications of the fact that parents and family form by far the greater part of the normal human environment of a child for several years, and that they are almost the whole of that environment during the first months and years of life, when the foundations of character are being laid.[1]

It is only too true that the vital and psychologically complex family relations may easily be distorted or even poisoned by the frailties or the vices, the weaknesses and the jealousies, of one or both of the parents, with the most disastrous effects on the children. But here we are concerned not with the psychopathology of the family figures, on which there is now an abundant literature, but rather with their essential positive functions and especially with that of the father in relation to his children.

The family is the first close association of people that the child knows and is therefore the prototype of the many different kinds of community of which he will or may become a member—his school, church, trade or profession, the armed services, as well as various societies, clubs, or other organizations he may join for different purposes; and finally his national community. It is in the family that he first learns to get on—or to quarrel—with other people, to find his own place among his fellows, and to obey the rules under penalties, at the lowest of disapprobation, at the highest, in the adult national community, of imprisonment, expulsion or capital punishment.

All communities, of whatever kind, whether school, church, army, tribe or nation, consist of members many of whom may be more or less equal in status, but in all large

[1] The disturbance or even abrogation of this relationship during the first years of a child's life under current industrial conditions in which many mothers spend most of their days at work outside the home is a grave and dangerous social innovation.

communities there is differentiation of functions or classes; and the community is frequently subject to a hierarchy, or several different hierarchies, subordinated to an actual or titular supreme head or leader—headmaster, pope, general, chief, president or king. In more primitive communities the leader or chief may enjoy power over the community which is absolute, but it is usually subject to limitations; while in others the real power has been taken over by a substitute, by an oligarchy, by a council, parliament or cabinet, or some other kind of executive body. But there can be little doubt that in the most primitive communities power is personal and at first inheres in the leader alone, perhaps in the most primitive of all through physical strength, but mainly through ability and force of character, or at last (more precariously) through the prestige deriving from traditional status. Of these various kinds of community the family is the prototype.

In the family the father is the natural leader or chief, and for long enjoyed—at least in the patriarchal social organization with which we are most familiar—absolute power over his wife and children; though in course of time the more civilized communities have limited that power through the force of public opinion and of custom, and eventually to a considerable extent by law. But his potential psychological dominance remains, just because he *is* the father, though it is of course greatly increased when he has force of character; and it is effectively supported if, as is still commonly the case, he holds the power of the purse and the responsibility for maintaining the family home. There are, it is true, deviations from this typical relation, as for example among Malinowski's Trobriand islanders, where the mother's brother is the father-substitute and governs the family. In a good many cases the mother has taken over a large part, sometimes the whole, of the father's power, because of his weakness or because she is of dominant masculine character. In very many families the power is shared between the two parents, by tacit or even explicit agreement, and there is often an accepted, and indeed natural, distribution of authority between father and mother in the different spheres of family life.

All these variations result from particular conditions of social and family life or from particular circumstances of character or aptitude, and underlying them all there is a basic psychical relation of children to their father. A primary cause of this relation is no doubt the fact that the father is normally the head and sustainer of the family, who stands in the closest relation to his children, and he naturally has the masculine prestige of the adult male in authority. How far the knowledge, conscious or unconscious, that he is the author of their being, that without him they could not have come into existence, contributes to the attitude of children towards their father is not easy to determine. Considering the apparently complete loss of psychical dominance suffered by the father in cases of early estrangement, and his frequent effective replacement by another figure, it would seem that such knowledge may be irrelevant, and that the actual psychical conditions of the first years of life are always the real determinants of the child's attitude. However this may be there can be no doubt of the reality of the father's psychical dominance in the typical case where he is the actual working head of the family.

Into the complex emotional relations of children to their father, about which Freud and other psycho-analysts have written so much, we do not propose to enter here in any detail. We may take it that children both give love to their father and need love from him, and that alongside this love there exists in varying degree a hostile attitude, potential at least, but capable of becoming very prominent and sometimes rising to the pitch of a very real hate. Both these sentiments are evidence of the strength of the emotional bond which unites children with their father. When they are at all evenly balanced, alternating in consciousness, sometimes at very frequent intervals, we speak of the affective relation as *ambivalent*. It is difficult for many people who are not familiar with the results of modern psychology to believe in the co-existence in one mind of such directly opposed sentiments towards the same person. It may be remembered however, that this co-existence has often been clearly recognized in the primary sex-relation between man and woman—that hostility, sometimes violent, may precede falling in love with a person of the opposite sex, and that not a few men both love and hate their wives, and not a few women their husbands. The hate sentiment, either for parent or spouse, is of course often repressed more or less completely because it is painful and may be deemed immoral as well, but of the reality of ambivalence there can be no doubt. Naturally the hate sentiment is fostered by bad treatment on the part of the object of the sentiment, just as love is fostered by consistent kindness, but neither owes its origin to the behaviour of the person involved. They are the opposite faces of a strong emotional relationship, initiated by the need of the individual self both to give and to receive love and by its capacity for hate.

When the child leaves the family home and becomes a member of other communities his psychical relations to his fellow members, and to the leader, are built up on the pattern of the family relations. At first these community relationships are relatively weak and may remain so indefinitely, but when a particular community comes to mean much in the psychical life of the individual they may rival or even excel in intensity the family bonds. The number of different communities that a man may enter is almost unlimited in the complex social structure of modern civilizations, though many of them, of course, are of quite minor psychological importance. We will here consider three, two of which—the church and the army—Freud discusses in his study of 'mass psychology', while the third is the national community to which the individual belongs.

The Christian church is taken in the sense of the religious body which the individual member actually recognizes, whether this is limited to his particular 'sect' or extends to the whole body of professing or practising Christians. The head of such a community is clearly God, who is thought of as the Father of the whole community and of each of its individual members. In the Trinitarian doctrine Christ forms a direct link with God the Father because He is both the Son of God and was made man by the Incarnation.

The parallel with the human family is close. The primary relation is one of love; first the love of God to man, perfect and all-embracing, a father's love which extends to every human being; and secondly the reciprocal love of man to God, weak and imperfect with the weakness of the undeveloped child, but capable of increasing perfection by the grace of God working through the Holy Spirit. Especially in the Roman Catholic church the Virgin Mary largely supplies the individual's need of a maternal figure. The idealized family relation is completed by the brotherhood of the members of the church—potentially the brotherhood of man—between whom there subsists, or should subsist, the universal relation of brotherly love.

Man can offend God, as the child can offend its father, originally by his 'first disobedience' and continually thereafter by 'sin'. But he can be reconciled to God by repentance, and the Father's love persists and never diminishes whatever the sins of the children. Man also 'fears God' as many children 'fear' their father, with an emotion quite different from hate, and in which awe and reverence are strong elements. But there are some people who actually develop hatred of God.

The army is a community of quite a different kind, organized for a specific purpose which naturally determines many of its characteristics. But several features of military organization resemble those of the family. In the first place the soldiers of an army actually live together like the members of a family. Then the Commander-in-Chief is in some sense the father of the army. Loyalty to him and his orders is a first condition of success in war, and warm affection vivifies and enhances loyalty. The better the acceptable General is personally known to his army through constantly coming among and talking to his men the more he knits them together into an effective instrument of his will. Many of the best commanders really love and are loved by their men, though there have been some excellent generals who do not.

In the army there is, of course, a very complete hierarchy of command with the function of leadership delegated by continuous steps from the commander-in-chief to the non-commissioned officer. Each of the lower units of command is in a certain sense a family, most conspicuously perhaps (in the British army) the regiment and the platoon—the former because of its strong and deep-rooted tradition, symbolized by its colours, the latter because it is small and personally manageable in action by one leader, so that all its members know one another well and can act closely together: the good platoon commander may be a real father to his handful of men. In the regiment the loyalty and affection of its members goes more to the unit as a whole, which is, as it were, personalized, than to its leader the colonel, and here we encounter that transference of love and loyalty from the leader and the actual members to the idea of the community as a continuing whole with constantly changing personnel which is met with in many types of community.

The modern national community, being so large and consisting of such a mixture of people of all kinds and all modes of life, has less of the characteristics of a family than the church or the army. But there is a sense of oneness, shared by all or most of its members, often unconscious, but conspicuously rising to the surface in times of national crisis and

particularly in time of war. And there is a titular leader—
king or president—who may be looked upon as a genuine
father of his people, though his powers in modern states
are strictly limited by the constitution of the State, and sometimes he may be not much more than a figurehead.

The existing English monarchy is an interesting case in
point. The King or Queen has practically no direct legal
power of any importance, though the sovereign may, in certain matters, or on certain occasions, exert a useful per-
suasive influence on his ministers in whom the executive
powers are vested. But the relationship of the British sovereign
to the people is very real and effective. Not only does the
Crown serve as a bond between the nations of the Common-
wealth and the colonies and dependencies of the Empire,
there is a personal relation between subjects and sovereign,
compounded of loyalty, respect and affection, and felt by the
great majority of the people. The loyalty depends primarily
on the prestige of kingship and the feeling that the sovereign
symbolizes the unity of the nation, while the respect and
affection must rest largely on the character and conduct of
the individual king or queen; but each emotion reinforces the
others, for the personality of the ruling monarch cannot be
wholly separated from his status as sovereign. The varying
degrees and shades of these emotions are well illustrated by
the attitudes of the English people towards successive sover-
eigns during the last century and a half.

Thus the relation of sovereign and people has certain of
the same qualities as that between father and children. Naturally there can be no personal contact between the sovereign
and the vast majority of his individual subjects, but there *is* a
personal *relation*, though it is mainly mental and imaginative,
supported by descriptions of his doings, by his speeches,
broadcasts and messages, by photographs, and by glimpses of
the person and demeanour of the sovereign on public occasions. The feeling of the nation as a family is also buttressed

by the characteristic domestic life of the English Royal family, with which the domestic life of the typical British family can be identified, though their styles are naturally far enough apart. The same is true of the Scandinavian countries and of Holland, the nations whose constitutions and ways of life are most closely akin to our own.

Much of the emotion originally attaching to the herd-leader, however, is not given to the monarch but is transferred to the nation thought of as a whole, in some sense personalized, and often mentally represented by the actual land of Great Britain, 'the country', with the totality of its inhabitants; and the positive feeling for this mental entity is what we call *patriotism*. 'Patriotism,' said Dr Johnson, 'is the last refuge of a scoundrel.' That may be true enough: the same might be said of religion or even of love itself. The finest and holiest emotional ideas may be used by mean and base egoism as screens to camouflage, though often unconsciously, the false position of the egoist in the world of human life; and the love of country is just such an emotional idea. On the other hand it may be the inspiration of self-forgetting service and devotion, and it is certainly a motive force which may save a nation from destruction in times of great peril. Just as the king may be thought of as the father of his people, so a man's native country is his fatherland, or alternatively his mother-land, for the country itself, its very earth, is a universal symbol of the mother. The images of his parents, the dominant influences of his formative years, symbolized by king or country to which filial love has been partly transferred, are maintained throughout life.

The community to which so many family emotions may be transferred was originally built up from an aggregation of families living close together and forming a clan. Its further evolution has taken many and diverse paths, depending partly no doubt on the particular heredity of the community but very largely on its habitat and the culture and economy resulting from heredity *plus* habitat, together with its contacts with other communities, its victories and defeats, its successes and failures in the world. The history of an isolated community living for centuries cut off from the great movements and migrations of peoples is naturally very different from that of one which has had constant intercourse with its neighbours through trade or war, through conquest, occupation, or peaceful immigration. The western nations on which most of our discussion has been based are of course examples of particular origins and histories and a consideration of native communities in Asia or Africa would have a different colouring and complexion. But the principle of leadership and dominance, based first of all on the adults with whom the young child is associated and later transferred to chiefs and other prominent figures in the adult community, is necessarily universal because it is ultimately based on the human child's original weakness and defencelessness in its long period of development, and of course on the fact that man is a gregarious animal who needs leaders if his community is to work effectively.

The gregariousness of man has often been attributed, as by McDougall, to a 'gregarious instinct', but until the conception of such an instinct has been further analysed and elaborated it is not very illuminating. It is to Wilfred Trotter and to Freud that we owe a considerable elucidation and extension of the conception. The 'gregarious instinct' implies only the individual's instinctive compulsion to associate with his fellow men. Trotter's 'herd instinct' relates to the individual's *specific sensitiveness to suggestions arising from the herd to which he belongs*, and the consequent formation of his beliefs and the direction of his actions according to the pattern of the opinions and codes of conduct shared by all (or most) members of his herd. These beliefs and opinions and codes of conduct are accepted by the average man as *right*, and are rarely subjected to criticism. They have 'the same *a priori* character, the same quality of utter convincingness, as beliefs based on other instincts, such as that good food or an attractive member of the opposite sex are desirable things.'[1]

Thus we must include the herd instinct among man's basic instincts. It exhibits all the characters of a typical instinct, as was shown in Chapter 5. The human mind has been moulded by the gregariousness of man. He is not only bound to associate constantly with his fellow men, he is also bound (within certain limits, it is true) to share their beliefs and their rules of conduct because he is utterly dependent upon his herd.

Freud, however, pointed out[2] that neither Trotter nor other writers on 'group psychology' had considered the all-important rôle of the herd leader; and mainly as a result of psycho-analytic work we can now see that the child develops his adult herd instinct through his early membership of his family, and that his father is his original herd leader. As he grows up his family herd is largely succeeded by his tribal herd, and in the later civilizations by his national herd, his 'occupational herd', and often by his political party, or by one of a number of other herds of which the Church and the Army are conspicuous examples. In each of these two last, as Freud points out, there is a supreme leader, who takes the place of the father; and we have seen that the common pattern is strikingly illustrated in both. In many cases however, the original loyalty and affection to the father is largely or wholly transferred to the herd itself, often because there is no conspicuous personality as leader. The herd beliefs and ideals become the beliefs and ideals of the individual member, and they are rarely submitted to rational criticism or judgment. The violently conflicting 'ideologies' of political parties,

[1] *The New Psychology* (1920), p. 222. Chapters XX and XXI of that book contain a fairly full discussion of Trotter's 'herd instinct', the original exposition of which is to be found in his *Instincts of the Herd in Peace and War* (1916).

[2] *Massenpsychologie und Ichanalyse* (1920) translated as *Group Psychology and the Analysis of the Ego*.

so conspicuous in the world today, are excellent examples of
this process where his political party is a man's most effective
'herd'.

We must conclude that herd instinct is an inherited disposition or instinct in the human race based on its necessary
gregariousness. It is moulded by the child's earliest life,
adapting him to his place in the family, and later on as a grown
man to his place in the various communities of his adult
world.

Note on Terminology. A number of different words have been
used by various writers on social psychology, often as syn-
onyms, for the human aggregations discussed in this chapter,
and this diversity of terminology is not conducive to clearness
of thought. Freud consistently uses *Masse*, which corresponds
pretty exactly with the English *mass*; but many recent English
and American psychologists have preferred *group*, a fashionable word which has unwisely been used to translate Freud's
Masse. It is not at all a good equivalent: *mass* stresses the incho-
ate nature of a collection of human beings in which their
separateness as persons is deliberately ignored; *group* is properly applied to an 'assemblage of persons, animals or material things standing near together so as to form a collective
unity: a knot (of people), a cluster (of things)' (*Oxford Dic-
tionary*). Relative *fewness* and *distinctness* of the objects forming
the group, as well as their collectivity, are certainly conveyed
by the word. No one in ordinary talk would naturally call the
inhabitants of the United States as a whole or even of Switzer-
land or Belgium a 'group'. Neither 'mass' nor 'group' is a
good designation for an organized *community* of human beings.
'Mass' is properly used when we are thinking of a human
aggregation as a body subject to forces conceived as imper-
sonal, neglecting personal relations which cannot be neglected when we are considering the structure and evolution
of a community. Trotter's *herd* stresses the biological aspect

of a community, its common instinctual equipment, and is useful for that purpose, while *community* stresses its organization as a whole.

It may be argued that these distinctions can be ignored, and that the particular word used does not really matter. But the implications and 'overtones' of a word taken from ordinary language always affect and may easily distort the impression made on the mind of the reader or listener: due attention should be paid to them by a writer or speaker in his choice of terms.

CHAPTER 11

THE INDIVIDUAL AND THE COMMUNITY

IN THE last chapter we have seen that the family is the psychological prototype of the adult human community though its members are united by specific and much closer bonds which are not, of course, repeated among adult members of a tribe or a nation. In the latter the individual acquires a new and independent relationship to his fellows which the growing child obviously cannot possess within the family framework.

As we saw in earlier chapters we may legitimately think of a 'herd instinct', an outcome of man's gregarious nature, which is the essential mental bond giving the individual man and woman *psychological* membership of his or her community. This conception, developed by Wilfred Trotter and given wide publicity in his well known book,[1] was not enthusiastically received either by academic psychologists or by psycho-analysts. The reluctance was partly due to current vagueness in connotation of the term 'instinct' which led many psychologists to discard it altogether; largely, on the part of psycho-analysts, to concentration of interest on deriving man's social relations from sexual and family origins; and to some extent at least to the almost universal disinclination of specialists to adopt ideas from non-professional sources. Nevertheless a great many people of intelligence who were not psychologists did welcome the conception because it obviously corresponded with the well known attitude of the average individual towards the beliefs and prejudices of his community. Up to a point a parallel attitude towards a new concept may be found in the widespread non-professional

[1] *Instincts of the Herd in Peace and War* (1916).

welcome that greeted the conception of the 'inferiority complex', based on Adler's work, which, like that of herd instinct, corresponded with a mental disposition constantly met
with in everyday life. Critical analysis of both concepts is of
course required.

Reasons were given in Chapters 5 and 10 for concluding
that 'herd instinct' is a valid and useful conception, 'instinct'
being understood as a type of psychological phenomenon in
accordance with McDougall's exposition. Without doubt the
adult response of the individual to his 'herd' is built up in
the individual life from the experiences of childhood in the
family, though it must have a hereditary basis correlated with
the gregarious habit, for no amount of 'training' will ever
qualify a non-gregarious animal, such as the domestic cat, to
become a member of a herd.

Herd instinct then, based on the specific sensitiveness of
the individual herd member to suggestions arising from the
herd, we shall take to be the dominant psychological motive
force, binding the herd together and regulating social attitudes. 'Fear of public opinion', not only fear of the social or
material consequences of a hostile public opinion, but also
strong aversion from being 'out of step' with the general
beliefs and attitudes of the herd, is one aspect of this dominant
instinct. On the positive side the normal individual wants to
be at one with his community, to be not only in it but of it. The
community that affects him most strongly and immediately is
composed of the people with whom he habitually associates,
his friends or his fellow workers. One must recognize that
a man may 'belong' to several different 'herds' at one and the
same time, and according to the circumstances of his life one
or other of these 'partial herds' may play the chief part in
determining the direction of his herd or social instinct. For
example, in a modern western nation it may be his com-
panions in the workshop, the local branch of his trade union,
or the body of his professional colleagues, the members of his

college, church or club, or of any society to which the individual belongs and whose objects are a controlling influence
in his life. For the professional politician and for all to whom
active party politics is a dominant interest it is very likely to
be his political party.

Then, of course, there are the 'partial herds' formed by the
stratification of the national community into 'social classes'
depending most commonly, though by no means always, on
family incomes or on education, and on the differences in
ways of life and opportunities which these determine. In many
respects this stratification is the most powerful of all the factors in differentiating 'partial herds' within the nation, and it
was even said by Disraeli that there are really 'two nations'
in this country—the 'under-privileged' and those who have
the means of a reasonably full and comfortable life. Both
classes show the phenomena of herd instinct in a marked degree, and the age-old conflict between them, sometimes
marked by bitter hostility, is too obvious and well known to
need elaboration. Communism and the more extreme forms
of socialism envisage an end to this state of things and the
establishment of a society in which *all* the members of his
nation—or even all mankind—would be the natural 'herd' of
the individual. Efforts to bring about a more even distribution of wealth by differential taxation, by limitation, and in
the last resort abolition, of profits, and to establish equality
by giving the opportunity of a better and uniform education
to the masses of the people, are seen as progress towards the
realization of such an ideal egalitarian national society.

But the forces making for stratification and segregation in
any large community cannot be nullified in this way. Privilege
will always establish itself, whether it depends on accumulated
wealth or on the necessary differentiation between those who
govern and those who are governed, and between those who
hold the more responsible and better remunerated positions
in the community and those who do not. Such differentiation

and privilege will always lead to the creation of partial herds within any large national community. So also will the close association of fellow workers and of all who have identical interests differing from those of other members of the national community.

More remote in its effect, except in times of acute national emergency such as a dangerous war, is the influence on the individual of the whole national herd as it exists at present in large and complex nations. In normal times this is too diffuse and composed of too many divergent interests and currents of belief and opinion for it to have as much power as his immediate associates in affecting the individual. The means of communication of national herd feeling and opinion, even when these are relatively well consolidated, are more indirect and therefore weaker than those of daily personal intercourse, though popular newspapers and latterly the radio may be used to influence wide sections of the people. Deliberate propaganda may masquerade as the genuine voice of the herd, but it may often be recognized for what it is and its effect largely nullified. In times of real emergency, when there is a dangerous and obvious threat to the safety of the nation, national herd instinct with its accompanying emotion of patriotism becomes immediately evident throughout the country, and the response to it, shown by the desire to *serve* the community, is overwhelming. Class conflicts, as well as individual egoisms, with their ugly accompanying emotions, lose much of their effectiveness, and the national herd becomes a real working super-organism through the activity of the common instinct in the great majority of the people.

Powerful and ubiquitous as are the manifestations of herd instinct there are, of course, co-existing urges in the individual mind which conflict with herd instinct and may prevail over its effects. First of all there is the crude self-regarding instinct of self-aggrandisement (which may become definitely anti-social), and then the sexual instinct, which is apt to rebel violently against herd prohibitions that are designed to regulate it. Either of these may easily overcome the normal effect of herd instinct in keeping the individual's conduct within the limits of the moral code held by society. But more interesting in the context of this discussion are certain higher developments of the individual mind.

The two most important of these are concerned respectively with ethical and intellectual convictions. The herd code of morals varies a great deal in different communities—'the wildest dreams of Kew are the facts of Katmandu, and the crimes of Clapham chaste in Martaban'. It also varies from time to time in the history of any given community. On the whole it is well adapted, like other tribal rules, to the particular community at the particular period of its history when it first took shape, though it often persists, like some other adaptive characters, after conditions have changed. It is clear that the herd must have *some* moral code and must do its best to enforce the code upon its members, or there would be moral and social chaos. As we saw in Chapter 2 the child normally learns his morals from his parents, who have themselves been inoculated with the moral code of their herd, so that there is formed in the child's mind what psycho-analysts call the super-ego; and that is the foundation of conscience, which troubles the adult individual if he disobeys its promptings. But in the sense adopted in this book the formation of a properly developed adult conscience demands the co-operation of reason working on adult experience, though the introjected foundation is indispensable. There must be ethical intuition—the profound conviction that this is fundamentally right and that fundamentally wrong—which is felt as unique —and this intuition has its origin in the super-ego formed in early childhood. By itself, however, the super-ego is a blind force which may prompt to actions remote from any rational appreciation of an adult situation, sometimes with disastrous results. The conscience developed from the super-ego with the aid of reason enables the individual to pursue a line which may depart from the herd code of morals. And it is the ultimate authority of the ethically responsible person. As McDougall has written, 'Conduct on its highest plane is regulated by an ideal of conduct that enables a man to act in the way that seems to him right regardless of the praise or blame of his immediate social environment'. Such conduct holds its own, if necessary, against herd instinct which would prompt the man slavishly to follow the herd's moral code.

To turn from ethical to intellectual convictions, a clear recognition of the vital importance of objective truth is certainly not a *primary* function of the human mind. High valuation of objective knowledge and general recognition of objective truth in regard to the external world of nature—by which is meant the kind of knowledge and truth obtained by observation, comparison and experiment and admitted as valid by all normal minds when the relevant data are fully understood and appreciated—was only attained by the western leaders of thought a few centuries ago. The necessary foundations were of course laid as soon as human consciousness was established, at first through repeated contacts with those fragments of the external world that are of immediate practical importance to the individual, contacts which gave him sufficient understanding of those fragments to enable him to control them or to direct his own attitude towards them in the interests of his first essential needs—for food, shelter and protection. The beginning of this power is seen, of course, in the higher animals (Russell's 'animal inference'—intelligence as contrasted with simple instinctive action), but was developed to a far higher level along with the increasing complication of the human brain. From such beginnings came the rudiments of natural science, at first directed mainly to dealing with the parts of the environment that directly concerned the individual and the community, but soon extended more widely,[1] so that an independent interest in understanding nature was created.[2] The development of scientific investigation was sporadic in the early civilizations, though at certain times and places it reached a high level in some departments of knowledge—a conspicuous example was geometry and astronomy among the Greeks—and it only attained full conscious expression in very recent centuries. With it came the realization that increase of objective natural knowledge by exact observation and experiment, and the formation of scientific concepts which could be tested by observation of fresh examples, not only greatly increased man's power of dealing with phenomena which directly concerned him in a material sense but led to the building up of a body of scientific theory that gradually enabled him to interpret natural phenomena at large more and more fully. This in its turn led to enormously increased power to control the natural world, and to the discovery of wholly new ways of dealing with human needs more quickly, economically and efficiently, and so to the industrial revolution which has created modern material civilization.

The new philosophy of nature that established itself in western Europe in the sixteenth and particularly the seventeenth centuries profoundly affected the intellectual attitude to scientific knowledge and ultimately to human problems. It was essentially based on a wide extension of the method of close observation and experiment in acquiring secure knowledge of the external world, and it was this of course which

[1] The members of some savage tribes are very good naturalists and do not confine their observations to what concerns their own personal needs.

[2] Of course there was also a great deal of superstition about nature, created by the strangeness and the frequent dangers of the external world under primitive conditions of life, by emotional factors, and by human proneness to fantasy. This proneness is very persistent in spite of gradually increasing objective knowledge, and hinders its development. It is still strong today, even among peoples who claim to be civilized. But human superstition and attitude to magic is of course an immense and complicated subject which can only be mentioned here.

created modern science. The widespread pursuit of natural science, enormously increased of recent years, has immensely fostered the urge to seek objective knowledge and the sense of loyalty to objective truth when it has been found. The instinct of curiosity pursued along intellectual paths— 'the exploratory function of the individual' as it has been called—was turned to close investigation of nature, and because of its extraordinarily successful and satisfying results, both intellectual and practical, it has led to the appearance of what amounts to a new type of mentality and to the unique and overwhelming prestige which now attaches to natural science. The methods of science have been systematically extended during recent times to the study of man himself, of the communities which he forms and the activities they carry on, and thus have arisen modern anthropology, modern psychology, sociology and economics. These are branches of science which of necessity largely lack the sovereign tool of controlled experiment and whose conclusions and theories therefore remain less secure than those of the physical sciences, but whose results do at least open new outlooks and more intelligent approaches to the human problems of the modern world.

The modern vogue of science is not without its drawbacks and dangers. The growth of new scientific knowledge has been so overwhelming that it has tended to dazzle men's minds and to obscure other human values, while the results applied to the satisfaction of material needs and desires have concentrated attention on practical applications and their effects in 'raising the standard of living' in the material sense, and have thus encouraged the growth and spread of a purely materialistic outlook upon life. Furthermore, a great deal of the detailed labour necessary to work out these applications is of a routine character well within the capacity of quite limited minds, and this has led to the creation of a large class of workers identified with the pursuit of science, and gaining some prestige from the fact, but of narrow vision which largely ignores other aspects and values of life and mind. In these directions lie the most serious dangers of modern science to any worthy modern civilization—far more than in the fundamental discoveries which have made possible the creation of terribly destructive weapons whose use on a large scale would destroy or at least place in peril the whole material and social framework on which civilization rests. That specific danger is real and threatening enough, but it can only be averted by an increase in the strength and extension of a world conscience. Pursuit of new knowledge leading to such discoveries cannot be permanently arrested when it has once excited men's imaginations, apart from having brought such rich material rewards in its train. But the worst danger to civilization is that of spiritual deterioration through the spread of false ideals or through the weakening of all ideals.

We have travelled far from the smaller and less complex European communities of medieval centuries when the structure of society was not only simpler but more stable, when everyone had, or at least was supposed to have, his own place and status in the social scheme. Codes of conduct were well established and generally accepted, and they were protected, in Western and Central Europe at least, by a religion whose truth and validity as an adequate sanction was almost universally accepted, a religion directed by a church that had no serious rival and thus possessed unique authority. There were tyrannies, wars and conquests, revolts and massacres, of course, and much sordid corruption, not to speak of pestilences and famines: there were also magnificent artistic cultures and great spiritual movements. The heights and depths of human virtues and vices were very much what they are today. But the human drama was played on a stage with less scenery and equipment, where a great deal was taken for granted, where common beliefs and assumptions guaranteed a relatively high degree of stability in the course of everyday life; and such conditions were maintained for many centuries.

The Reformation movements weakened the Catholic Church, restricting or abolishing its authority over wide areas of Europe, the Revival of Learning with its enthusiastic study of the works of classical antiquity, side by side with the new urge to investigate nature by objective methods which led to the beginnings of modern science and its new philosophy of nature, geographical discoveries of new and distant lands, and the opening up of North America to European colonization—all these, while they immensely widened man's intellectual scope, tended to disrupt the stable organization of the older societies.

But it was the industrial revolution that followed, brought about by the wide application of the results of scientific work to the easier and more efficient satisfaction of human needs and desires, that brought about the greatest transformation in the social organization of Western Europe, first in England and then on the Continent, gradually changing the bulk of the population from rural to urban, and largely replacing the farmer and the peasant by hosts of workers in the new factories. In spite of the continued high death-rate, though it gradually diminished through improved sanitation and medical knowledge, the pace of growth in the population increased enormously through the great accretions of material wealth, and during the nineteenth century the English people came to depend on food produced in developing oversea countries, largely paid for by the export of manufactured products.

It was inevitable that this basic change in the balance of the population and its economy should bring about, with increasing pressure for democracy, a potential shift of political power to the industrial wage earners, a shift made actual in the nineteenth century by successive extensions of the electoral franchise and the ultimate granting of universal suffrage. The concentration of the great majority of the people in towns and cities made close political organization much easier, while the formation and legalization of trade unions furnished a ready means of bringing working men together for the advancement of their interests. Originally established to secure higher wages and improved conditions of work, the unions have come to take a direct interest in politics, and in Great Britain the formation of the Labour Party and its eventual accession to power have given them a powerful influence on Government. This influence, aided by the leadership of 'intellectual' socialists such as the Fabians, has been increasingly directed during the last half century to the advocacy and support of thoroughgoing socialistic legislation.

It is, of course, quite remote from our purpose to discuss party-political or economic questions as such: we are only concerned here in so far as they spring from, and in their turn affect, the psychological attitude of the individual to the community.

There is a well-marked human tendency to adopt, and to press, extreme views, especially when they become embodied in the tenets of a political party or of a religious sect. The ebbs and flows of such extreme views are expressions of Bergson's 'loi de la double phrénésie', well rendered by Arnold Toynbee as 'man's frantic way of going to opposite extremes alternately'. Authoritarianism and libertarianism, asceticism and licence, strict religious dogma and 'free thought' are examples of such alternations which have often been illustrated in history. All three of these pairs may be regarded as expressions of the two contradictory human needs—for discipline and for freedom—in all spheres of individual and social life. In the philosophical sphere a similar alternation of contradictions is the 'thesis' and 'antithesis' of the Hegelian (and Marxian) dialectic. To the place of the 'synthesis'—the ultimate term of the dialectic—in the process we shall have occasion to recur.

In our British political life the alternations of Whig and

Tory, Liberal and Conservative, in Government (particularly of Liberal and Conservative during the later nineteenth century, and in the twentieth Socialist and Conservative) accompanying the advance of democracy, were examples of the successive swings of the political pendulum. The pendulum did not necessarily reach an extreme height on either side and there were often considerable irregularities due to differences in current economic, social and international circumstances, or to the appearance of particularly able and forceful political personalities who deflected for a time the regular sequence of the swings. During the period of democratic development there was, however, a continuous 'leftward' trend among the leaders of political thought, so that the actual tenets and policies of the radicals of one generation became those of moderate conservatives in the next. But the swings of the pendulum continued to occur because they were the expressions of deeply rooted human needs.

When we turn to the concrete content of the successive opposite movements, to the topics with which they are actually concerned, we find that during the Victorian period the Liberal emphasis was on increased freedom—the freedom of the individual—which was to be extended to the wage-earning class (since the wealthier part of the population were already free in many respects simply because of their money) and it was expressed in various measures of social reform and especially in the extension of the franchise. Conservatives avoided far-reaching changes as much as possible. But in present day politics the line of division is quite different. On the whole the line separates two opposite conceptions of the proper organization of society, generally known as socialism and individualism. The matter is complicated however, by the controversy about the legitimacy of the private capitalism which has been so extensively developed in the most prosperous of the modern industrial countries, and has in fact been one of the principal agents of their great increase in wealth.

F

Of course private capitalism is radically opposed to socialistic
doctrine, but it is quite possible to imagine an individualistic
society in which interest on private capital (unless perhaps
on loan to the State) was forbidden, and we cannot forget that
usury was condemned in medieval society as contrary to
Christian morality. We cannot in fact *identify* a capitalist with
an individualistic society. Nevertheless the freedom to accumulate capital and to lend it at interest may well be regarded as
indispensable to a successful non-socialistic industrial society
and there seems no reason to hold that rents and interest, with
suitable adjustments and safeguards against extortion, are
repugnant to sound ethics.

The extreme socialistic view, however, not only condemns
private interest-bearing capital, but regards the 'profit motive' as immoral and holds that it should be replaced by the
motive of 'service to the community.' On the other hand the
individualist holds that honestly made profit represents a useful activity which is psychologically indispensable to the most
effective and economical production. The extreme individualist position, is that all legally acquired private property is
sacrosanct. The underlying general position of the Socialists,
in its extreme development, which ultimately becomes
frankly totalitarian, is that the interests of individuals must
always give way to those of the State. The opposite 'Liberal'
view is that protection of the interests and the liberty of
individuals is the main consideration of importance in domestic policy.

The psychological motives behind such extreme views are
instinctive and emotional. They are either the expressions of
a primary instinct or of a 'negative' emotional urge aroused by
the frustration of such an instinct. It is the violence of the
reaction of frustration that often gives these urges their sinister force. Moderate politicians and 'centre parties', which at
least try to balance different human needs against one another
and to avoid 'slogans' that spring from and arouse strong feel-

ing, nearly always tend to be squeezed out of existence between the upper and the nether millstones of the extremists, because they lack the fierce energy of passionate emotion.

The ultimate sources of the belief in the liberty of the individual, including the liberty to compete freely with others in all the activities of life, are self-regarding instincts, crystallized in what is called 'self interest', the urge to magnify the self, to increase its power and status and to satisfy its desires. If a man can win for his wife a particular girl whom he desires in competition with other men he has, it is agreed, the right to do so, and if he can gain trade which would otherwise go to his neighbour by giving more efficient service, or even by skilful advertisement, he has equally the right so to gain it. If he can obtain a good position by beating his competitors in an examination, by showing better qualifications for a job, or by making a good impression on a prospective employer, he is at liberty to do it and is applauded for his success. The spur which such goals exert on an individual is thought to increase his initiative and efficiency and thus the aggregate efficiency of the community by stimulating its individual members. This is no doubt a rational basis of the belief in the advantages of free enterprise and free competition. At the same time success on these lines clearly enhances what McDougall calls 'positive self-feeling', and thus gives satisfaction to the individual. The belief in the maintenance of this way of life, in free enterprise and free competition, with a large measure of liberty for the individual to do what he likes, and what he can, with his own life, is shared to a great extent by the peoples of the western democracies and is, or has been, most notably characteristic of the United States, where it may be said to be incorporated in the herd code of *mores*, though its ultimate springs, as we have seen, are self-regarding instincts. Thus the 'American way of life' has the double support of self-regarding and herd instincts. It is *right* because it not only gives individual satisfaction but also gains social (and, as we saw in Chapter 5, also divine) approval.

The psychological forces which conflict with the 'free' way of life in a western democracy are more complex. Primarily they represent the revolt of the 'underprivileged' wage earners, the demand for higher incomes, better conditions of work, and more leisure, the conditions of a more comfortable and a fuller life—improvements which the Liberals of an earlier generation strove to effect by social reform backed by an extended franchise, but which Socialists believe can be brought about more effectively by changes in the economic structure of society involving the abolition of private capitalism. In addition to this revolt from below is the widespread emergence of what is now often called the 'social conscience'. Social conscience in an individual, in its widest meaning, is the sense of responsibility for other members of the community. It is part of the desire for unity with the herd which gives rise to herd instinct and is ultimately based on sympathetic identification with other people. The individual not only desires to conform to the beliefs and *mores* of the herd, but also, so far as he can, to promote the well-being of its other members. Those who are favourably situated often have a strong sense of *guilt* for the circumstances of their fellows who suffer from poverty or bad conditions of life.

In the conditions of modern industrial civilization it has become increasingly evident that freedom to compete, at least in individual private enterprise, theoretically open to every individual citizen, is largely unreal because the fields of competition are too closely occupied by great organizations which command most of the capital resources necessary for success in the modern business world. Here and there a newcomer can make good, but there remain great numbers of people who cannot get their feet on the lower rungs of the ladder which might lead to individual success. The result is that the vast majority of the population remain as wage earners with no prospect of real independence, and often below the poverty line.[1] This is clearly a totally different type of society from that of early nineteenth century America, for example, where a sparsely populated country rich in natural resources gave opportunity to any able and adventurous man to make his own way in the world. The change in Great Britain and other European countries, whose economies were more stable, more complex and more highly developed, has been in the same direction. In all such countries many of the people who were comfortably off, both those who had successfully made money and those who lived on the interest of inherited wealth or on the rents of inherited property began to feel that something drastic ought to be done to improve the conditions of life of the vast numbers of 'underprivileged'. The 'social conscience' was aroused. Many and various steps were taken to mitigate these evils, by private charity, by voluntary organizations, and by legislation such as the various poor laws and schemes of public assistance. But none of these attacked the roots of the evil. Sporadic private charity was felt by many to be insulting to the wage earner and in any case could not relieve more than a minute fraction of existing distress. The old poor laws were oppressive in many ways and sometimes positively cruel, while permitted public assistance was quite inadequate to deal with the problem at large. Better wages and conditions of work began to be demanded as a right, and even with good wages repugnance to working for the profit of private employers increased.

In these conditions the doctrines of Socialism began to appeal to increasing numbers of people—not only under-

[1] Hence the original function of the labour unions, with the ultimate weapon of the strike in reserve, which present continual demands for higher wages, compensating to some extent, though inadequately, for the impossibility of embarking on an independent career in which a man is his own master and may be able to increase his income indefinitely. In any case of course, a large number of wage earners is essential to massive industrial production whether their wages are paid by private employers or by the State.

privileged wage earners but people of independent means who could not possibly profit from such a change—as the proper remedy for the economic ills of society. Grinding poverty side by side with great wealth and luxury, selfishness and oppression on the part of many employers of labour, recurrent mass unemployment which put the wage earner at the mercy of his employer, large profits from the labour of underpaid workmen, increasing monopoly in trade and industry nullifying the freedom of competition boasted of by individualists—why not replace an economic system which produced these crying evils by a benevolent State system directed by a government given power by a majority representing those who were suffering? Why not 'nationalize' 'the means of production, distribution and exchange', transfer them to State ownership, so that the employees became servants of the nation and their grudging contribution to the wealth of greedy capitalists would be replaced by the feeling that they were working for the community? And why not replace the incentive of profit making by the desire to serve the community, by pride and satisfaction derived from good work done for its own sake, and by the hope of promotion in a great State organization?

The moral prestige attaching to these ideals is obvious, and it is certainly true not only that some of the current socialistic legislation has removed serious injustices and gross inequalities, but that the motives of many who have devoted themselves to the cause of socialism were, and are, pure and fine enough. But there is a good deal to be said on the other side. In the first place it is more than doubtful if the suggested psychology is sound, for example if the profit motive can in fact be effectively replaced for the majority of people by the motive of service to the community; and again if the State as employer, for more than one reason, can ever satisfactorily replace the private employer in its relations with its employees in many of the spheres of industry that are involved.

And behind the splendid moral façade of socialistic ideals, there are often motives which are far from lofty in the minds of many socialists who have suffered from existing conditions and of some who are actuated by sheer envy of the means which give independence. It is as if they said 'We cannot all be rich, so let us deprive people of independent means of as much as possible of their resources by the heaviest possible taxation and death duties. If I cannot have this desirable thing I will at least see that no one else shall.' The plain malice that sometimes accompanies this attitude is unmistakable.

Envy—one of the meanest of human motives—is certainly one of the roots of the egalitarianism which is often preached as necessary to 'social justice'—a term by which different people mean different things. In spite of the vagueness of its connotation it is habitually used, even by writers who ought to know better, without any attempt at definition. Some people mean by it the greatest possible equality of income, status, and absence of privilege for all citizens. Such an ideal clearly excludes the right to 'make money' (and invest it) privately—a form of freedom which has never in practice been denied in modern western civilization, but which involves of course the hated 'capitalism'. Taxation and death duties which are heavy enough are effective means towards the end contemplated. But even in a community from which the freedom to accumulate wealth has been removed and everyone lives on what he earns from the State, absolute equality of means and privilege is clearly impossible, if only because of the very different qualifications necessary for different callings and the very different ways of life that these callings necessarily entail. The work of the nation cannot be carried on with anything like equality of incomes. A Socialist State must differentiate widely between the wages it pays to its employees. But if the truth of this thesis would be generally admitted by Socialists, inherited wealth and the accumulation of private capital remain anathema. As to status and privilege, they will always re-establish themselves in human societies, however completely you may have destroyed the old 'privileged classes' by depriving them of the possibility of their old ways of life. Status and privilege are always and necessarily accorded to those who have *power* of any kind, and an equal distribution of power throughout a community is even more impossible than an equal distribution of income. A comprehensively egalitarian society is in fact out of the question.

There is, however, another meaning of social justice, and that is *equality of opportunity*, which is a very different thing. Considerable advances have already been made towards the provision of free opportunity for different kinds of education, especially higher education and technical training in preparation for corresponding careers; and these should, and no doubt will, continue till young people from every class who are suitably qualified by natural talent will never be hindered by lack of means or opportunity from pursuing any kind of career they may choose. Equality of opportunity has nothing to do with socialism or individualism. It increases the dignity and freedom of the individual by giving him or her a greater chance of leading a full and well adapted life, and at the same time places more inborn talent and trained skill at the disposal of the community.

Just as we can clearly trace a mixture of envy and a lofty ideal in current socialistic propaganda, so we can find in much so-called individualism a blend of the noble and the base. Assertion of the right to individual freedom unhampered by a network of prohibitory laws and restrictive regulations comes from an instinct which is the primary spring of constructive human endeavour; but it may also lead not only to a weakening self-indulgence but to a claim to the liberty to exploit one's fellow men to their serious detriment in one's own selfish interest.

The old antagonism between the 'haves' and the 'have nots' has taken different forms at different times. Today the conflict which splits the nations, and indeed the world, has a specific form. It is a struggle between those who want to maintain the 'free society', giving as much liberty as possible to the individual compatible with social order and the avoidance of obvious abuses and injustices, and those who believe that the interests of the individual should always give way to those of the State, however seriously State interests may injure the individual's own. This basic difference of belief really depends on different conceptions of what the 'State' is, or should be. By the one party it is conceived of as a central organization *with limited functions* in a community of people inhabiting a defined geographical region, a community which by history and tradition have a common fatherland and resulting common habits and loyalties. Its functions of external defence, maintenance of internal order and the removal of gross injustices, are intended to secure conditions which enable all the people, as individuals, to secure to the fullest extent the enjoyment of 'life, liberty and the pursuit of happiness'. This is the American ideal embodied in the constitution of the United States, and until very recently, though less explicitly, the British ideal too. By the opposite party the State is conceived of as a kind of super-organism which inevitably comes to have interests of its own that may easily conflict with the interests of individuals. When such conflicts occur the individual's interest must always give way to the State interest, however much his liberty and his pursuit of happiness may thereby be impaired.

It is true that 'State interests' are always represented as 'national' or 'common' interests—common, that is, if not to all the people, at least to the majority, who have returned, by their votes, a socialistic government to power. The interests of the minority, however large and important the minority may be, are ignored or deliberately injured. What these so-called common or national interests actually are, and how they can best be advanced, is in any case necessarily decided by the small number of men composing the government, and even with complete good will, at least to their own supporters, they cannot always be trusted to decide rightly and wisely. The machinery of election to Parliament is in fact, and perhaps unavoidably, very clumsy indeed, and the application of the doctrine of 'mandate' from the electorate at a general election is subject to constant dispute. It is true of course that this consideration applies to all democratically elected governments whatever their political complexion, but its effect is enormously increased when the government policy is to enact an immense mass of complicated legislation affecting the economic interests and everyday life of all the people.

The great complexity of the economic structure and of the innumerable activities carried on by the people of a modern industrial nation, when the detailed regulation of these activities is made the concern of the central government, involves a corresponding complexity of the executive side of government, an enormous civil service which becomes a bureaucratic hierarchy of great elaboration and great power. In its well-meant efforts to promote what is supposed to be the common interest the government is forced to enact an increasingly voluminous series of laws issuing in thousands of bureaucratically devised 'regulations' which seriously hamper the individual in many of his ordinary everyday activities. By the time the enactments supposed to represent the 'will of the electorate' as expressed by the vote of the majority returns to the individual elector, through the triple process of election, legislation and administration, in the form of regulations which direct his conduct under legal penalties, the result may easily show a wide discrepancy from, and even directly contradict, his real will and desire, even when these are conscious and definite. Meanwhile the interests of important minorities whose work is of real value to the community are neglected or destroyed in the effort to cater for the real or supposed needs of the majority. The concentration of such wide-ranging and drastic power in the hands of Government and of the civil service separates its exercise too far and too completely from the individual citizen. The Government claims to 'represent' the nation, but when it undertakes to devise a planned economy and regulate it in detail in accordance with a particular political and economic theory, its degree of separation from the people themselves is so great that the 'State' (i.e. the Ministers plus the Civil Service) becomes a separate entity with interests of its own which are quite distinct from those of the people, and in which not only administrative convenience but the enjoyment and enhancement of power may often play an important part.

Much of what has been written has become the commonplace of current Conservative (and Liberal) criticism of socialistic legislation and administration, but some description of the ways in which the political and administrative machinery of socialism works has been necessary for a consideration of its psychological effects on the individual citizen. The first of these effects is largely due to the harassment of the individual as a result of the enormous multiplication of regulations of all kinds having legal force. Many of these are looked upon by a large proportion of the population as trivial or vexatious, or both, and are widely evaded or disregarded. Breaches of them are often due to ignorance, since it is practically impossible for the individual citizen to become acquainted with all the regulations which may affect him personally. Others are known and wilfully disregarded if it is believed that legal penalties can be evaded. The English have a good reputation on the Continent as a law-abiding people, but the habit of constantly doing things which are actually illegal inevitably breeds disrespect for law as such. The same tendency is seen in the increase of sudden 'unofficial' strikes, which are sometimes actually illegal, and in any case are officially opposed by the trade union of which the strikers are members. The men complain that the union officials are dilatory in instituting negotiations or are out of touch with their needs, just as many citizens complain that Whitehall officials are out of touch with theirs.

The annoyance of vexatious regulations affects all citizens. Those concerned with the management of commercial and industrial undertakings feel in addition serious frustration in many of their necessary managerial activities. Some of the chains in which they are bound are no doubt necessary as a consequence of the present economic position of the nation, but most are in any case essential to the working of the socialistic organization of a planned economy. The middle and upper classes suffer hardship, which is often very severe, as the result of the excessively heavy taxation necessary to maintain the extravagantly organized 'Welfare State' and this is especially burdensome to those who have to live on fixed incomes derived from investments. Many Socialists of course hold that such people should not be allowed to exist. On retirement from work they should all live on State pensions.

The total result is that almost the whole population have grievances of one kind or another, often exceedingly bitter grievances, and the fact encourages lawlessness and discourages public spirit. There is widespread deterioration of the national psychology in its attitude to the State.

The second psychological effect is due to the 'Welfare State' itself, or rather to the way in which it is organized, and an outstanding example is the British National Health Service. Most people would agree that some kind of National Health Service was a most desirable thing, and the existing service has undoubtedly given much needed relief to very many people. The valid criticism (apart from serious defects in its medical organization) is that it is undiscriminating and does not confine its work to those who really need medical help for which they cannot afford to pay. This is another example of the almost pathological and ultimately futile passion for egalitarianism. The ease with which everyone can now obtain medical benefits in the widest sense for themselves and their families, whether they can afford to pay for them or not, inevitably weakens the incentive to assume personal responsibility for the care of the family and therefore weakens the family bond, which is largely sustained by the sense of responsibility to its members. When State benefits of every kind can be had for the asking there is little need for the cardinal positive virtues of initiative, sense of responsibility, and the practice of thrift. The effect upon character can hardly be worse. There is no doubt that the virtues of thrift were excessively praised by the Victorians. With some natures saving money easily becomes an end in itself, so that the true function of money is entirely distorted; and an ingrained habit of 'saving' is often allied with very unpleasant qualities of character of which miserliness is the most obvious. But the practice of thrift, properly exercised, is still a most desirable adjunct to most lives, especially when it is specifically directed to securing future objects more worthy and desirable than those which can be obtained by current spending. Universal State benefits tend to put thrift out of action altogether.

Until either private interest-bearing capital is entirely eliminated and a completely socialistic State established, or a different approach is made, Disraeli's 'two nations' will continue to exist, though the wealth and power of one of them has been very greatly diminished and bids fair to be destroyed altogether. In a completely 'socialized' State another division of society will be formed—that between increasingly numerous official government servants who receive the higher incomes and the necessary accompanying privileges, and the wage-earning remainder of the population. This is seen in its extreme form in Russia today, but something like it must arise in any socialistic State with a completely planned economy. Whether that division will make for a more harmonious nation may well be doubted, judging from our brief experience of the effects of the first steps in the new direction. There is no reason to suppose that pressure for continually increased incomes for the wage-earners will diminish, and it is clear that they cannot be afforded by the nation without greatly increased production at home and continuous access to foreign markets in which products can be sold at remunerative prices—neither of which can be guaranteed. Meanwhile the possibility for the individual of attaining financial independence will have disappeared, except perhaps in some subordinate spheres considered to be not worth 'nationalizing'. The 'free way of life' will have vanished or almost vanished.

On the other hand we cannot possibly now return to the old regime in its entirety—nor would it be desirable if we could, for it harboured many abuses and inflicted much hardship. Can a middle way be found which may perhaps preserve at least a reasonable degree of individual freedom and may lead to a greater contentment among the people at large, and a healthier attitude towards the State? There is no evidence that the average working man, pleased at first by the access to power of a Labour government pledged to socialistic legislation which he thought would benefit him, is at all satisfied with present conditions. He still talks about 'they', as opposed to 'we', when he speaks of the actions of authority. Would he be any more pleased with completely socialized industry in which his freedom would be no greater, if as great, as it was? Instead of being able to bargain with a private employer he will be up against the supreme power of the omnicompetent State. Alternatively, in some of the 'nationalized' industries he will be able to intimidate the Government by threatening to suspend essential public services. In either case disastrous conflicts must ensue.

In the ideal democratic State all the citizens should think of national actions as 'our' actions, but at most that is now only possible when the nation is at war, and to some extent in the sphere of foreign policy. It is doubtful if it will ever be completely possible in the modern complex industrial community because the interests of different sections will remain divergent, even if the property-owning class wholly disappears.

The redistribution of national income has gone far to eliminate the gross contrasts between great wealth and luxury and extreme poverty, though the taxation of the middle as well as the higher incomes has been unduly severe and has caused a great deal of real hardship. The interests of important though numerically small sections of the community have been injured or neglected. Genuine social justice would try to attain some reasonable balance between different interests, hard though the task might be. The life of the country in its widest sense is made up of the activities of all sections of the community, and so far as these are not grossly wasteful, like some of the extravagances of the very wealthy, or obviously harmful, like the activities of criminals, they should all be tolerated and not persecuted. This is the essence of freedom in its deepest sense, so far as it can be secured externally, and only in this way can the richness and variety of the life of the nation, which are the real glory of any country, be maintained and extended. The springs of that richness and variety depend on the activities of individual men and women, or of small groups, not on anything the State can do.

These considerations bring us back to the conflict between individualism and socialism and to the relation between the individual to his herd in terms of the modern complex industrial nation. It is impossible on the one hand to escape from the fact that humanity consists of individuals and nothing else, and that all human action therefore depends in the first instance exclusively on individual activity. The widest possible freedom to exercise it is an essential condition of national vitality. On the other hand man is a gregarious animal, his normal everyday life is in the society of his fellows, and only through continuous co-operation can he defend himself against attacks from without, maintain a peaceful and law-abiding society and make progress towards the realization of a harmonious community. It is clear enough that he can never reach perfection in this last respect—human beings are too various in their mental make-up ever to agree completely on the relative importance of different human values. The only solvent öf such differences is toleration of other people's values and interests. Toleration is an all-important social and political virtue.

Democracy at best is a clumsy and imperfect method of government, but it seems the only safeguard against tyranny of dictators and oligarchies. The rule of a government 'representing' a majority of the people is thus inescapable if a country is to remain free from individual or oligarchical tyranny, but it must not oppress or persecute minorities in the supposed interests of its majority or it becomes itself a tyranny. What has been called 'empirical liberalism' is the only healthy political doctrine. This, as has recently been said, does not necessarily exclude all socialistic legislation, but it should be limited to those spheres in which it shows a clear balance of economic and national advantage. Doctrinaire and of course vindictive legislation should be wholly avoided. Wide regions of competition with opportunities for that strong psychological incentive, the profit motive, must be retained. Incentives to initiative and imaginative originality as well as to good honest conscientious work cannot be spared. A central government's legitimate functions, in addition to defence and the preservation of social order, are now by general agreement admitted to be the securing of a minimum necessary income for all good citizens, and at the same time the necessary conditions for a maximum of opportunity and of individual liberty to use it must be secured. Restrictive legislation and detailed regulations involving meticulous regimentation should be reduced to an absolute minimum.

Along such lines lies the best chance of prosperity, contentment and happiness for the individual and a *feeling* of freedom together with oneness with his national society. In such a way we should have something to correspond with the dialectical 'synthesis'—in this case inevitably a compromise or halfway house—between the thesis and antithesis of individualism and socialism, albeit a synthesis which the good Marxist could never approve, just because it *is* a compromise!

World federation and world government are magnificent ideals but necessarily remote ones. It is amazing how easily idealistic internationalists seem able to ignore the stupendous obstacles to their realization, when we consider the present profound diversity of national and tribal character, culture and sentiment, as well as of social and economic structure. At present the problem can only be attacked piecemeal, and what is called 'functionally', but we shall do well no doubt to keep the ultimate ideal—a real 'world herd' should that ever be possible—always in mind.

CHAPTER 12

PSYCHOLOGICAL REALITY AND SPIRITUAL VALUES

IT WAS said at the end of Chapter 1 that we cannot escape from the psychological reality of *spiritual values*, which are of a totally different nature from material values, and that this is the reason why man has always thought of these values as concerned with a distinct part of himself which he calls his soul or spirit, and which he feels to be not only the highest part of himself but the very core of his being. On the plane of natural science we cannot discuss the nature of the soul nor even affirm its existence as a separable entity, but we must recognize the psychological reality (what Russell has called the 'psychological inevitability') of spiritual values and we cannot agree with those who contend that it vanishes on analysis.

By a psychological reality we mean a recurring inescapable idea in the mind, an idea that is as convincing to its possessor as any of those based on external reality of which he has constant experience through his senses. Such ideas vary indefinitely in their incidence. In the extreme case they may be limited to single individuals, as when a madman is convinced that he is Napoleon Bonaparte or Adolf Hitler or God; on the other hand they may be shared by vast numbers of people. It is obvious that ideas which are limited to individuals whose minds are seriously distorted and who have lost touch with external reality can have no validity except to the individuals possessing them; but those which are shared by many people have an increasing validity the more widely they are believed in.

It may be argued that this contention makes validity (or 'truth') depend on a mere counting of heads, that it is parallel with the view that the opinion of the majority is always right;

but such an argument confuses different kinds of validity or truth. It is clear that we must distinguish, for example, between scientific truth and artistic or religious truth.[1] A characteristic of scientific truth is that it is accepted by all who are capable, or can be made capable, of understanding the evidence; and this potential capacity is to all intents and purposes universal. But that is not true of artistic or of religious truth. The appreciation of beauty in nature or in art or in both is widespread but not universal, and for the recognition of what is meant by artistic truth a particular type of mind, and often a particular training, is required.

It is notorious that men differ profoundly on what they mean by religious truth, that the bitterest wars have been fought in the name of divergent religious convictions, though it has been fairly said that there is little real religion in the minds of the fighters. And there are some who hold that all religion is an illusion. Nevertheless the vast majority of the human race imperatively need *some* kind of religion—a fact that is witnessed by the formidable spread of Communism in recent years, side by side with a widespread decay of the Christian faith. It is precisely because Communism *is* in one sense a religion, because, like all the great religions, it enables a man to transcend his individual interests (while it is supposed at the same time to meet the claims of natural science) that it has succeeded in commanding the adherence, and even the devotion, of millions.

It is generally agreed that Communism takes root and flourishes where there is widespread economic misery, and we can find a parallel in the rapid spread of Christianity among the slaves of the Roman empire. In Roman times this new and intense faith in the infinite love of a supreme God with the hope of a blissful after-life gave consolation and compensation for the bondage and the frequent material misery of the

[1] We must leave to philosophers the problem of the common element which justifies the use of the word 'truth' for all three.

individual slave, while to the freeman it represented much higher spiritual values than most of the current pagan religions of the earlier Greco-Roman civilizations with their galleries of gods and goddesses who could scarcely be respected as individual figures and were no longer taken very seriously by the educated citizen. Today the ideal of Communism with its future Utopia of a classless society where there would be no gross inequalities of wealth and in which everyone would find contentment in working for the whole community, not only promises material security and thus to relieve those who are now materially wretched, but also makes a spiritual appeal to many high-minded idealists whose compassion for the poor and needy are a good deal stronger than their knowledge of the potentialities of human nature. Many such people cannot tolerate the existing chaos and widespread suffering in the world and they feel that the universal adoption of Communism would reduce society to order—as of course it would if it were successfully established and could be permanently maintained, though at the cost of all individual freedom. Idealistic communists are frustrated in their spiritual aspirations for universal good will and happiness just as the materially wretched are frustrated in their primary desire for a life that would give them a sufficiency of the basic needs of physical existence.

If we set aside the people who join the Communist movement for what they can get out of it and those who see in its organization a chance of obtaining power over their fellow men, these material and spiritual frustrations are at the bottom of the impulse to become a communist. Frustrations that are unendurable and seem unescapable, have a profoundly devastating effect upon the mind. Parental love and protection for the young child are one of the first conditions of sound psychical development, and their deprivation is well known to lead to mental trouble and disruption of character in later life. The early histories and adult mentalities of many 'intellectual' communists reveal similar causes at work. Their adult personalities are often definitely psychopathic, displaying a marked rift in the mental make-up. Among them are men of great intelligence and some of really brilliant intellect, and they may also be quite capable of various normal human relationships, but the moral sense of the typical member of the Communist party is completely distorted, so that some of the cardinal virtues of common humanity, such as ordinary loyalty and good faith are repudiated and replaced by a desperate fanaticism which takes supposed advantage to the Communist cause as the sole guide to right conduct. The only loyalty is to the Cause: all other duties are, or may be, disregarded. Extreme examples of such disrupted minds have come to light in recent trials for treason, but this condition of what has been called psychic 'compartmentalism' is very widespread among communists, and very naturally leads to increasing distrust of all members of the Communist party, because of its ominous threat to the moral and social order of the civilized free world.

The power of dividing the mind into compartments in which different standards and ways of thought obtain, and which are 'logic-tight' and 'emotion-tight', is a very common psychical phenomenon. Such division is never of course, compatible with the psychical integration which is essential to wisdom and virtue alike, and it is mortally dangerous when emotion and conation are concentrated in a typical fanaticism of which the modern communistic creed is the most striking current example, The danger is particularly formidable because of the form Communism has taken in the organization of a Great Power and its satellites, to whose behests the Communist parties of almost all other countries are subservient. It is perfectly possible to *imagine* an innocuous communist community free from the cruelty and bad faith of the government which we see exemplified in countries in which the Communist party has seized power, though

whether such a community could ever become a viable state
in the modern world without the ubiquitous activities of
secret police is an unanswered question. But it must be freely
admitted that some of the changes effected under communist
regimes have really benefited the masses of the people in
certain respects, and the people are not without gratitude.

Meanwhile there are many idealistic people who profess
the Communist creed but are quite free from the sinister type
of moral disruption—William Morris was a conspicuous example—and we may conjecture that their adoption of the
underlying ideals of communism has still been due to early
frustrations of spiritual aspirations, for which adherence to
these ideals proves a kind of compensation. Clearly the
expression taken by the creed of an individual must be largely
influenced by his actual mental make-up. In its religious
aspect the communistic creed may ideally be a fine thing,
though in its actually dominant form today it is truly a
Satanic creed, because it repudiates the beliefs and values
inseparably associated with the great traditional religions and
practises almost every form of bad faith, unscrupulous cruelty,
and oppression. However fine its ultimate ideals may be, their
pursuit by such means can never be justified. Totalitarian
tyranny, denial of all human freedom, in itself stultifies any
conceivable ideal.

Psychological reality is a fact of the individual mind and
does not, in itself, depend in any way on how widely it is
shared by other minds. But when particular ideas are very
widespread in the human race they do by that fact establish
a claim to validity, simply because their recurrent existence
can only mean that the human mind is so constituted as to
generate these ideas again and again, that many or most minds
cannot, so to speak, get along without them. And the ideas
to which spiritual value attaches are outstanding examples.
They are enshrined in the great religions of the world, but

their influence extends far beyond the circles of professed believers. They may be analysed, and their origin and nature described in non-spiritual terms by scientific philosophers, but their ultimate validity is not impaired by such perfectly legitimate and often useful exercises in analysis. Love is a supreme example of the highest spiritual value, and the reality and overwhelming importance of love is in no way diminished by such an analysis as that which was attempted in Chapter 8.

What then is the status of these spiritual values in terms of human life considered as a product of evolution? We can never understand the nature of the human mind if we ignore its origin from the minds of our animal ancestors who were not yet human.

It was maintained in Chapter 5 that the human mind is dominated by a complex of inherited instincts derived from those of sub-human ancestors whose nearest living non-human descendants are the anthropoid apes; but the expressions of these instincts are often so altered, and sometimes so distorted by conflict with other instincts and by the effects of the enormously increased complexity of the human brain and of life in human society as to render them difficult of recognition except as a result of psychological analysis on modern lines. Among these primitive instincts there is one which is very old biologically, going back, as we saw in Chapter 8, to almost the simplest living beings—the impulse of the organism to union with something outside itself which is the basis of love. Beginning in human life with the love of the child for its mother, on whom the infant depends for every need, and finding its primary adult expression in the mating instinct of the great majority of animals, the impulse to union in man extends far beyond the specialized functions of sex to include human beings other than the mate, even to the whole human race, and ultimately reaches up to the love of God and the intense desire for union with Him. On these higher levels love is the supreme spiritual value.

There are schools of thought which hold that an analysis of love that traces its origin in organic evolution back to primitive biological impulse destroys its spiritual significance. This view is very often associated with lack of belief in the existence of God, but it may equally be held by professed believers, including ecclesiastics, who fear the slow sapping effect of natural science, especially of biology and modern psychology, in undermining religious faith. At one extreme analysis is welcomed as destructive of superstition, at the other it is condemned as subversive of religion, but both parties agree on its effects.

It cannot be denied that a frequent effect of scientific analysis is to destroy faith in the existence of God. But it is more than doubtful if people who are thus affected ever had any genuine realization of the nature of His Being—or at least of what that nature is *not*. It should be obvious enough that the existence of God is not on a par with that of the objects of the natural world which we perceive through our senses, though many people do not understand the distinction. The confusion leads to bad philosophy, and bad theology too. 'God is a spirit, and they that worship Him must worship Him in spirit and in truth'.

Unless man possessed the impulse to union based on his essential biological nature he could never have experienced family affection, nor the feeling of union with and loyalty to his society or community, flowering in the emotion of patriotism, nor devotion to the ideal of a unified world, nor the pantheistic emotion which has characterized many of our finest minds, nor the conception of one supreme God with whom union is possible. These emotions and ideas could never have come into existence but for the impulse to a union originally physical but which can altogether transcend bodily union.

These things have *emerged* in the mind of man in the course of his evolution from a primitive state in which his special endowments were only just rising from the mental level of his anthropoid ancestors. In the historical aspect the conception of God, with Whom union is possible though it may be difficult, is the ultimate term of the progression which began with the impulse to physical union—originally of almost the simplest living organisms. The doctrine of 'emergence' propounded by certain recent philosophers is a possible key to this historical process. The great stages of evolution have been marked by the successive emergence of new entities, each of a different nature from preceding entities which formed their foundations. Thus chemical atoms presumably arose from the association of electronic particles, chemical molecules from unions of atoms of the chemical elements; living substance, and then individual organisms, have emerged from the association of particular complex molecules; mind has emerged from organic function; and the human spirit, possibly, from mind.

Of course religion claims far more than this. It claims that spirit is the ultimate reality, and Christianity claims that spiritual truths have been directly revealed to man. As to that natural science can say nothing whatever. It can neither affirm nor deny such propositions. But it can say that historically the psychological reality of spirit and spiritual values has emerged from mental function; and it is possible to conceive of spirit as *the underlying reality which only became manifest to man when his mind was sufficiently developed to become capable of perceiving spiritual values*. The difficulty in such a view lies in the unanswered question—what was the place of spirit in the universe during the ages before man appeared and became capable of perceiving spiritual values? The only possible answer would seem to be that spirit was necessarily latent until man could perceive it and that that was inherent in the Divine Plan. The scepticism of those to whom the results of science represent the whole of reality is intelligible enough. No one knows anything at all about possible manifestations of an ultimate spiritual reality outside the human mind on our earth. There may or may not be, or have been, other worlds than ours in which spirit became manifest. But we may be permitted to hold, with William Law, the English eighteenth century mystic, that 'the soul of man is an effluence from God' and that 'the essences of the soul have been in God from all eternity'.

The best evidence for the belief in spirit as the ultimate reality is derived from the phenomena of religious mysticism. The mystical vision and the experience of mystical union with God are unique phenomena which have been directly known only to a small proportion of the human race, but which are repeatedly recorded alike in the history of the old religions of the East and in the writings of the Christian mystics. The analyses of psychologists have attempted to resolve these experiences into conditioned components, but they have not destroyed their psychological reality nor their spiritual value, any more than the biological and psychological analysis of love destroys the reality and value of love. It may be that these realities and values are actually ultimate.

Thus two distinct conceptions of the nature of man exist in the world today, and it is obvious that they are radically different. One of these is the traditional belief, which has probably existed in some form, however crude, ever since man first began to think about his own nature. This is that he is essentially a spiritual creature, that over and above the existence of his living body and its material activities, he possesses a soul or spirit which is the core of his being and which is often held to survive his physical death. The other is the doctrine, which has grown up, especially in modern times, with the steady advance of biological and other scientific knowledge, that man is essentially an animal, though with unique endowments and powers, and that there is no valid evidence that he is anything beyond his living body whose wide-ranging activities have gradually developed and expanded from those of his pre-human ancestors. Many of those who hold this doctrine are convinced that *all* the activities of the living human being, like those of other animals, can ultimately be resolved into physical and chemical processes, though in some respects the essential biological processes are certainly *sui generis*. Even vitalists admit of course, and it has been abundantly demonstrated, that the detailed mechanism of the human body works according to the chemical and physical laws which are common to living organisms and inorganic matter.

It is clear that acceptance of the second view, with its common addendum, as a complete statement of the ultimate nature of man, amounts to acceptance of what is called the philosophy of 'materialism', though the suitability of the word may be questioned since modern physics has abolished 'matter' as one of the fundamental concepts and has substituted the concept of 'energy' as the ultimate physical reality, retaining the use of 'matter' for aggregations of the ultimate units of energy into atoms, molecules and larger entities and for its practical convenience in our dealings with the world of common sense and of the more elementary branches of science.

These refinements do not, however, concern our present discussion. We all know what is meant by materialistic philosophy—the denial of ultimate reality to anything other than the physical constitutents, whatever they may be, through which the universe works. In this conception of man both mental and spiritual 'phenomena' are regarded as outcomes of the physical processes set up in men's brains as the results of his contacts with his surroundings—some of them useful or indispensable to his existence, others harmless or harmful fantasies or illusions.

There are some however, who would not deny the psychological reality of spiritual values, but would dissent from the view that spiritual truth differs in kind from scientific truth. They would hold that spiritual values arise in men's minds by abstraction of principles of conduct from human experience and by the unconscious co-ordination of ideas concerned with the well-being of human societies. Thus spiritual values would have a purely ethical basis and would be an outcome of psychological evolution in the mind of a gregarious animal that had become capable of abstract thought in adaptation to his life in societies of very highly organized individual animals. As such, spiritual values would not only be susceptible, like other psychological phenomena, of scientific analysis, but they could be completely explained in this way. Clearly this mode of approach could not admit the mystical vision as evidence of the ultimate and independent reality of the spiritual sphere.

It is abundantly clear that unless we repudiate the results of natural science we must go a long way with the materialists, or rather the mechanists. There is the strongest evidence that the human race has arisen by degrees from pre-human animals and that man is still an animal, whatever else he may be. It is also true that when his bodily processes are success- fully studied in detail they are found to obey the general laws of chemistry and physics, just as are those of other animals. The human body is a mechanism—an immensely complicated mechanism with the most astonishing powers, but still a mechanism—dependent upon its particular structure, upon the properties of the materials of which it is composed and upon the energy with which it is supplied. We can, it is true, draw a line between living organisms and inorganic matter, pointing to the unique characteristics of life, but the argu- ments of the vitalists that these are of really basic significance have not convinced the majority of biologists. And the line between the living and the not-living is now considerably blurred by the discovery of the viruses, which are in many respects intermediate, possessing some, but not all, of the properties of living organisms.

However that may be, the question has no direct bearing on the nature of man, and of his differences from the higher non-human animals. The human mind is, of course, vastly superior to those of man's distant cousins the apes and of his even more remote relatives, the dogs and horses. Nevertheless the rudiments of many of man's mental characteristics, not only his emotions but his reasoning powers, can be traced in these animals. This fact, already demonstrated by animal psychologists, has been well brought out by Russell in his recent book on *Human Knowledge* in connection with what he calls 'animal inference', the basis of human inference.

Thus there is no sharp line to be drawn between the human race and the other higher animals, immense as the progression has been from one to the other, a progression in which the appearance of spoken language marked the biggest and most severing step. It seems that the whole of the evidence points to a continuous process of evolution, probably from the inorganic to the organic and then through a long series of stages (with many divergent lines and blindly ending offshoots) to the human species with its capacity for acquiring a detailed knowledge of the external world, for largely mastering and adapting its matter and energy to human uses, and for thus producing complex civilizations. During the whole process of evolution upon the earth a series of conspicuous advances, usually with disappearance of the immediately preceding stages, has led to the 'emergence' of what appear as completely new phenomena, of which the most conspicuous have been the advent of living organisms and, many hundred million years later, of the human race. We cannot be *certain* that this is a true account of man's origin and history in the world—no human knowledge with the exception of that represented by mathematical statements is really certain—but the accumulated evidence makes it difficult to refuse credence to the story.

It was argued at the beginning of this chapter that psychological reality, when it is shared by a large number of human beings, has an inescapable claim to represent one kind of 'truth', taking this word in its widest meaning. Nothing is more conspicuous in human history than the persistence among the most various races of man of the conviction that he possesses a soul or spirit which transcends his bodily existence; that he is, in essence, a spiritual being, of common nature with an ultimate spiritual reality lying at the root of all existence. It was suggested that the realization of spiritual reality emerged in the human mind as man's mental functions developed; and in this way it may be possible to accept both the conceptions of man's nature, radically different as they are—to hold, in effect, that he is *both* an animal, subject to biological and physical laws, and *also* a spiritual being.

Before the immense development of modern science took place it was natural for the conception of man as a spiritual being to stand in the forefront of the reflections of philosophers on human nature. To the great majority doubts of its truth scarcely occurred. But with the vast increase of our knowledge of the mechanisms of living beings and of the universe the impact of this knowledge upon human thought has been overwhelming, and has challenged the older deep-rooted conception. It is a challenge that is one of the greatest dangers of the contemporary world, for a universal denial of spiritual reality is almost certain to lead to universal catastrophe. For the majority of human beings there is no valid substitute for the 'Perennial Philosophy', whatever form it takes, as a secure spiritual anchor. The challenge cannot be met by a futile attempt to deny the validity of the results of science—it can only be met by fully accepting them and at the same time refusing to abandon the older view for which the evidence is internal to the human mind. The best hope of avoiding spiritual catastrophe lies in the widespread signs of religious revival in the midst of the flood of materialism.

The practical task is to re-assert spiritual truth in a form in which it can be assimilated by the mass of mankind, and that will be exceedingly difficult. The old symbolisms have largely or completely lost their value to a very large proportion of the more widely informed and materialistically minded people. Traditional religion tends to be replaced by the deadening philosophy of materialism, often, though not of course necessarily, allied with the social philosophy of Communism. And the quarrels of those professing religion have not helped to retain its hold upon the multitude.

We cannot *disprove* the view that physical forces exhaust the content of human life as well as of the material world, that mental and spiritual phenomena can all be not only 'explained' but 'explained away' by analysis in terms of biological, and ultimately, of physical, concepts—we can only have faith in spiritual reality as the result of a deep conviction within our own minds that we are spiritual beings as well as animals. 'Faith is the evidence of things unseen', but things that are none the less real.

GEORGE ALLEN & UNWIN LTD
LONDON: 40 MUSEUM STREET, W.C.1
CAPE TOWN: 58–60 LONG STREET
SYDNEY, N.S.W.: 55 YORK STREET
TORONTO: 91 WELLINGTON STREET WEST
CALCUTTA: 17 CENTRAL AVE., P.O. DHARAMTALA
BOMBAY: 15 GRAHAM ROAD, BALLARD ESTATE
WELLINGTON, N.Z.: 8 KINGS CRESCENT, LOWER HUTT

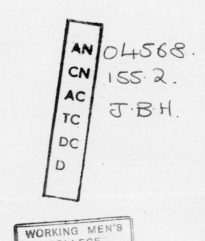